MW01708278

Just The

facts101

Textbook Key Facts

Textbook Outlines, Highlights, and Practice Quizzes

Surviving Your Dissertation: A Comprehensive Guide to Content and Process

by Kjell Erik Rudestam, 3rd Edition

All "Just the Facts101" Material Written or Prepared by Cram101 Textbook Reviews

Title Page

facts101
LEARNING SYSTEM

"Just the Facts101" is a Content Technologies publication and tool designed to give you all the facts from your textbooks. Visit JustTheFacts101.com for the full practice test for each of your chapters for virtually any of your textbooks.

Facts101 has built custom study tools specific to your textbook. We provide all of the factual testable information and unlike traditional study guides, we will never send you back to your textbook for more information.

YOU WILL NEVER HAVE TO HIGHLIGHT A BOOK AGAIN!

Facts101 StudyGuides
All of the information in this StudyGuide is written specifically for your textbook. We include the key terms, places, people, and concepts... the information you can expect on your next exam!

Want to take a practice test?
Throughout each chapter of this StudyGuide you will find links to JustTheFacts101.com where you can select specific chapters to take a complete test on, or you can subscribe and get practice tests for up to 12 of your textbooks, along with other exclusive Jtf101.com tools like problem solving labs and reference libraries.

JustTheFacts101.com
Only Jtf101.com gives you the outlines, highlights, and PRACTICE TESTS specific to your textbook. JustTheFacts101.com is an online application where you'll discover study tools designed to make the most of your limited study time.

By purchasing this book, you get 50% off the normal monthly subscription fee!. Just enter the promotional code **'DK73DW23768'** on the Jtf101.com registration screen.

www.JustTheFacts101.com

ISBN(s): 9781490274300. PUBX-4.20131123

Surviving Your Dissertation: A Comprehensive Guide to Content and Process
Kjell Erik Rudestam, 3rd

CONTENTS

1. The Research Process

CHAPTER OUTLINE: KEY TERMS, PEOPLE, PLACES, CONCEPTS

	Conceptual framework
	Empirical
	Research question
	Brainstorming
	Element
	Knowledge by acquaintance
	Knowledge by description

CHAPTER HIGHLIGHTS & NOTES: KEY TERMS, PEOPLE, PLACES, CONCEPTS

Conceptual framework	A conceptual framework is used in research to outline possible courses of action or to present a preferred approach to an idea or thought. For example, the philosopher Isaiah Berlin used the 'hedgehogs' versus 'foxes' approach; a 'hedgehog' might approach the world in terms of a single organizing principle; a 'fox' might pursue multiple conflicting goals simultaneously. Alternatively, an empiricist might approach a subject by direct examination, whereas an intuitionist might simply intuit what's next.
Empirical	The word empirical denotes information acquired by means of observation or experimentation. Empirical data are data produced by an observation or experiment. A central concept in modern science and the scientific method is that all evidence must be empirical, or empirically based, that is, dependent on evidence or consequences that are observable by the senses.
Research question	A research question is the methodological point of departure of scholarly research in both the natural sciences and humanities. The research will answer any question posed. At an undergraduate level, the answer to the research question is the thesis statement.
Brainstorming	Brainstorming is a group or individual creativity technique by which efforts are made to find a conclusion for a specific problem by gathering a list of ideas spontaneously contributed by its member.

1. The Research Process

CHAPTER HIGHLIGHTS & NOTES: KEY TERMS, PEOPLE, PLACES, CONCEPTS

	The term was popularized by Alex Faickney Osborn in the 1953 book Applied Imagination. Osborn claimed that brainstorming was more effective than individuals working alone in generating ideas, although more recent research has questioned this conclusion. Today, the term is used as a catch all for all group ideation sessions.
Element	In mathematics, an element or member of a set is any one of the distinct objects that make up that set. Writing A = {1, 2, 3, 4 },means that the elements of the set A are the numbers 1, 2, 3 and 4. Sets of elements of A, for example {1, 2}, are subsets of A. Sets can themselves be elements. For example consider the set B = {1, 2, {3, 4}}.
Knowledge by acquaintance	The distinction between 'knowledge by acquaintance' and 'knowledge by description' was promoted by Bertrand Russell . Russell was extremely critical of the equivocal nature of the word know, and believed that the equivocation arose from a failure to distinguish between the two fundamentally different types of knowledge.
Knowledge by description	The contrasting expressions 'knowledge by description' and 'knowledge by acquaintance' were promoted by Bertrand Russell notably in On Denoting, who was extremely critical of the equivocal nature of the word know, and believed that the equivocation arose from a failure to distinguish between the two fundamentally different types of knowledge.

CHAPTER QUIZ: KEY TERMS, PEOPLE, PLACES, CONCEPTS

1. The contrasting expressions '_________' and 'knowledge by acquaintance' were promoted by Bertrand Russell notably in On Denoting, who was extremely critical of the equivocal nature of the word know, and believed that the equivocation arose from a failure to distinguish between the two fundamentally different types of knowledge.

   a. Probability sampling
   b. Empty set
   c. Knowledge by description
   d. Image

2. . The word _________ denotes information acquired by means of observation or experimentation. _________ data are data produced by an observation or experiment.

   A central concept in modern science and the scientific method is that all evidence must be _________, or empirically based, that is, dependent on evidence or consequences that are observable by the senses.

a. Empirical probability
b. Endogeneity
c. Epps effect
d. Empirical

3. In mathematics, an _________ or member of a set is any one of the distinct objects that make up that set.

   Writing A = {1, 2, 3, 4 },means that the _________s of the set A are the numbers 1, 2, 3 and 4. Sets of _________s of A, for example {1, 2}, are subsets of A.

   Sets can themselves be _________s. For example consider the set B = {1, 2, {3, 4}}.

   a. Element
   b. Empty set
   c. Identity function
   d. Image

4. A _________ is used in research to outline possible courses of action or to present a preferred approach to an idea or thought. For example, the philosopher Isaiah Berlin used the 'hedgehogs' versus 'foxes' approach; a 'hedgehog' might approach the world in terms of a single organizing principle; a 'fox' might pursue multiple conflicting goals simultaneously. Alternatively, an empiricist might approach a subject by direct examination, whereas an intuitionist might simply intuit what's next.

   a. Growing block universe
   b. Grue and bleen
   c. Conceptual framework
   d. Knowledge space

5. The distinction between '_________' and 'knowledge by description' was promoted by Bertrand Russell . Russell was extremely critical of the equivocal nature of the word know, and believed that the equivocation arose from a failure to distinguish between the two fundamentally different types of knowledge.

   a. Probability sampling
   b. Empty set
   c. Knowledge by acquaintance
   d. Image

ANSWER KEY
1. The Research Process

1. c
2. d
3. a
4. c
5. c

---

2. Selecting a Suitable Topic

CHAPTER OUTLINE: KEY TERMS, PEOPLE, PLACES, CONCEPTS

____________	Statement
____________	Research question
____________	Variable
____________	Argument
____________	Brainstorming
____________	Contradiction
____________	Development
____________	Moderator variable
____________	Self-schema

CHAPTER HIGHLIGHTS & NOTES: KEY TERMS, PEOPLE, PLACES, CONCEPTS

Statement	In logic a statement is either (a) a meaningful declarative sentence that is either true or false, or (b) what is asserted or made by the use of a declarative sentence. In the latter case, a statement is distinct from a sentence in that a sentence is only one formulation of a statement, whereas there may be many other formulations expressing the same statement. Philosopher of language, Peter Strawson advocated the use of the term 'statement' in sense (b) in preference to proposition.
Research question	A research question is the methodological point of departure of scholarly research in both the natural sciences and humanities. The research will answer any question posed. At an undergraduate level, the answer to the research question is the thesis statement.
Variable	In mathematics, a variable is a value that may change within the scope of a given problem or set of operations. In contrast, a constant is a value that remains unchanged, though often unknown or undetermined. The concepts of constants and variables are fundamental to many areas of mathematics and its applications.

Argument

In logic and philosophy, an argument is an attempt to persuade someone of something, by giving reasons for accepting a particular conclusion as evident. The general structure of an argument in a natural language is that of premises (typically in the form of propositions, statements or sentences) in support of a claim: the conclusion. The structure of some arguments can also be set out in a formal language, and formally-defined 'arguments' can be made independently of natural language arguments, as in math, logic and computer science.

Brainstorming

Brainstorming is a group or individual creativity technique by which efforts are made to find a conclusion for a specific problem by gathering a list of ideas spontaneously contributed by its member. The term was popularized by Alex Faickney Osborn in the 1953 book Applied Imagination. Osborn claimed that brainstorming was more effective than individuals working alone in generating ideas, although more recent research has questioned this conclusion. Today, the term is used as a catch all for all group ideation sessions.

Contradiction

In classical logic, a contradiction consists of a logical incompatibility between two or more propositions. It occurs when the propositions, taken together, yield two conclusions which form the logical, usually opposite inversions of each other. Illustrating a general tendency in applied logic, Aristotle's law of noncontradiction states that 'One cannot say of something that it is and that it is not in the same respect and at the same time.'

By extension, outside of classical logic, one can speak of contradictions between actions when one presumes that their motives contradict each other.

Development

In classical differential geometry, development refers to the simple idea of rolling one smooth surface over another in Euclidean space. For example, the tangent plane to a surface (such as the sphere or the cylinder) at a point can be rolled around the surface to obtain the tangent-plane at other points.

The tangential contact between the surfaces being rolled over one another provides a relation between points on the two surfaces.

Moderator variable

In statistics and regression analysis, moderation occurs when the relationship between two variables depends on a third variable. The third variable is referred to as the moderator variable or simply the moderator. The effect of a moderating variable is characterized statistically as an interaction; that is, a qualitative (e.g., sex, race, class) or quantitative (e.g., level of reward) variable that affects the direction and/or strength of the relation between dependent and independent variables.

Self-schema

The term self-schema refers to the beliefs and ideas people have about themselves. These beliefs are used to guide and organize information processing, especially when the information is significant to the self. Self-schemas are important to a person's overall self-concept.

2. Selecting a Suitable Topic

CHAPTER QUIZ: KEY TERMS, PEOPLE, PLACES, CONCEPTS

1. In logic a _________ is either (a) a meaningful declarative sentence that is either true or false, or (b) what is asserted or made by the use of a declarative sentence. In the latter case, a _________ is distinct from a sentence in that a sentence is only one formulation of a _________, whereas there may be many other formulations expressing the same _________.

   Philosopher of language, Peter Strawson advocated the use of the term '_________' in sense (b) in preference to proposition.

   a. Term logic
   b. Tetralemma
   c. Train of thought
   d. Statement

2. _________ is a group or individual creativity technique by which efforts are made to find a conclusion for a specific problem by gathering a list of ideas spontaneously contributed by its member. The term was popularized by Alex Faickney Osborn in the 1953 book Applied Imagination. Osborn claimed that _________ was more effective than individuals working alone in generating ideas, although more recent research has questioned this conclusion. Today, the term is used as a catch all for all group ideation sessions.

   a. Probability sampling
   b. Cauchy's integral theorem
   c. Brainstorming
   d. Conformal welding

3. In mathematics, a _________ is a value that may change within the scope of a given problem or set of operations. In contrast, a constant is a value that remains unchanged, though often unknown or undetermined. The concepts of constants and _________s are fundamental to many areas of mathematics and its applications.

   a. Vinculum
   b. Y-intercept
   c. Variable
   d. ROARMAP

4. A _________ is the methodological point of departure of scholarly research in both the natural sciences and humanities. The research will answer any question posed. At an undergraduate level, the answer to the _________ is the thesis statement.

   a. Research spin-off
   b. Research station
   c. Response rate
   d. Research question

5. . In logic and philosophy, an _________ is an attempt to persuade someone of something, by giving reasons for accepting a particular conclusion as evident. The general structure of an _________ in a natural language is that of premises (typically in the form of propositions, statements or sentences) in support of a claim: the conclusion.

The structure of some _________s can also be set out in a formal language, and formally-defined '_________s' can be made independently of natural language _________s, as in math, logic and computer science.

a. Argument
b. Cauchy's integral theorem
c. Complex analytic geometry
d. Conformal welding

ANSWER KEY
2. Selecting a Suitable Topic

---

1. d
2. c
3. c
4. d
5. a

---

3. Methods of Inquiry: Quantitative and Qualitative Approaches

CHAPTER OUTLINE: KEY TERMS, PEOPLE, PLACES, CONCEPTS

- Empirical
- Empiricism
- Epistemology
- Rationalism
- Research design
- Case studies
- Logical positivism
- Hypothetico-deductive model
- Positivism
- Descriptive statistics
- Inferential statistics
- Randomization
- Sampling
- Variable
- Control group
- Posttest
- Analysis of variance
- Matching
- Multiple regression
- Interaction
- Paradigm

3. Methods of Inquiry: Quantitative and Qualitative Approaches

CHAPTER OUTLINE: KEY TERMS, PEOPLE, PLACES, CONCEPTS

Variance

Constructivism

Social constructivism

Methodology

Phenomenology

Coding

Heuristic

Emic

Grounded theory

Perspective

Narrative inquiry

Qualitative Research

Action research

Single-subject design

Data collection

Mixed model

Collection

Statement

Constructionism

Process theory

Meta-analysis

Empirical

The word empirical denotes information acquired by means of observation or experimentation. Empirical data are data produced by an observation or experiment.

A central concept in modern science and the scientific method is that all evidence must be empirical, or empirically based, that is, dependent on evidence or consequences that are observable by the senses.

Empiricism

Empiricism is a theory of knowledge that asserts that knowledge comes only or primarily from sensory experience. One of several views of epistemology, the study of human knowledge, along with rationalism, idealism, and historicism, empiricism emphasizes the role of experience and evidence, especially sensory perception, in the formation of ideas, over the notion of innate ideas or traditions; empiricists may argue however that traditions arise due to relations of previous sense experiences.

Empiricism in the philosophy of science emphasizes evidence, especially as discovered in experiments.

Epistemology

Epistemology is the branch of philosophy concerned with the nature and scope of knowledge and is also referred to as 'theory of knowledge'. It questions what knowledge is and how it can be acquired, and the extent to which any given subject or entity can be known.

Much of the debate in this field has focused on analyzing the nature of knowledge and how it relates to connected notions such as truth, belief, and justification.

Rationalism

In epistemology, rationalism is the view that 'regards reason as the chief source and test of knowledge' or 'any view appealing to reason as a source of knowledge or justification.' More formally, rationalism is defined as a methodology or a theory 'in which the criterion of the truth is not sensory but intellectual and deductive.' Rationalists believe reality has an intrinsically logical structure. Because of this, rationalists argue that certain truths exist and that the intellect can directly grasp these truths. That is to say, rationalists assert that certain rational principles exist in logic, mathematics, ethics, and metaphysics that are so fundamentally true that denying them causes one to fall into contradiction.

Research design

Research design is considered as a 'blueprint' for research, dealing with at least four problems: which questions to study, which data are relevant, what data to collect, and how to analyze the results.. The best design depends on the research question as well as the orientation of the researcher. Every design has its positive and negative sides.

Case studies

In the social sciences and life sciences, a case study is a descriptive or explanatory analysis of a person, group or event. An explanatory case study is used to explore causation in order to find underlying principles.

3. Methods of Inquiry: Quantitative and Qualitative Approaches

CHAPTER HIGHLIGHTS & NOTES: KEY TERMS, PEOPLE, PLACES, CONCEPTS

Logical positivism	Logical positivism, logical empiricism, or neopositivism embraced verificationism, a set of theories of knowledge that combined logicism, empiricism, and linguistics to ground philosophy on a basis consistent with exemplary examples of empirical sciences. Seeking to overhaul all of philosophy and convert it to a new scientific philosophy, the movement emerged in the late 1920s from the Berlin Circle and from the Vienna Circle. Appalled by Western society's flaring racism, bigotry, and nationalism, but perhaps no less by countermovements toward metaphysics, mysticism, and intuition, logical positivists were inspired by developments in mathematical logic, philosophy of language, and physics, especially general theory of relativity.
Hypothetico-deductive model	The hypothetico-deductive model, first so-named by William Whewell, is a proposed description of scientific method. According to it, scientific inquiry proceeds by formulating a hypothesis in a form that could conceivably be falsified by a test on observable data. A test that could and does run contrary to predictions of the hypothesis is taken as a falsification of the hypothesis.
Positivism	Positivism is a philosophy of science based on the view that information derived from logical and mathematical treatments and reports of sensory experience is the exclusive source of all authoritative knowledge, and that there is valid knowledge only in scientific knowledge. Verified data received from the senses are known as empirical evidence. This view holds that society, like the physical world, operates according to general laws.
Descriptive statistics	Descriptive statistics is the discipline of quantitatively describing the main features of a collection of data. Descriptive statistics are distinguished from inferential statistics , in that descriptive statistics aim to summarize a data set, rather than use the data to learn about the population that the data are thought to represent. This generally means that descriptive statistics, unlike inferential statistics, are not developed on the basis of probability theory.
Inferential statistics	In statistics, statistical inference is the process of drawing conclusions from data that is subject to random variation, for example, observational errors or sampling variation. More substantially, the terms statistical inference, statistical induction and inferential statistics are used to describe systems of procedures that can be used to draw conclusions from datasets arising from systems affected by random variation, such as observational errors, random sampling, or random experimentation. Initial requirements of such a system of procedures for inference and induction are that the system should produce reasonable answers when applied to well-defined situations and that it should be general enough to be applied across a range of situations.
Randomization	Randomization is the process of making something random; this means: Randomization is not haphazard. Instead, a random process is a sequence of random variables describing a process whose outcomes do not follow a deterministic pattern, but follow an evolution described by probability distributions.

Sampling

In statistics and survey methodology, sampling is concerned with the selection of a subset of individuals from within a population to estimate characteristics of the whole population.

Researchers rarely survey the entire population because the cost of a census is too high. The three main advantages of sampling are that the cost is lower, data collection is faster, and since the data set is smaller it is possible to ensure homogeneity and to improve the accuracy and quality of the data.

Variable

In mathematics, a variable is a value that may change within the scope of a given problem or set of operations. In contrast, a constant is a value that remains unchanged, though often unknown or undetermined. The concepts of constants and variables are fundamental to many areas of mathematics and its applications.

Control group

In the design of experiments, treatments are applied to experimental units in the treatment group (s). In comparative experiments, members of the complementary group, the control group, receive either no treatment or a standard treatment.

For the conclusions drawn from the results of an experiment to have validity, it is essential that the items or patients assigned to treatment and control groups be representative of the same population.

Posttest

Pre-test probability and post-test probability (alternatively spelled pretest and posttest probability) are the subjective probabilities of the presence of a condition (such as a disease) before and after a diagnostic test, respectively. Post-test probability, in turn, can be positive or negative, depending on whether the test falls out as a positive test or a negative test, respectively. In some cases, it is used for the probability of developing the condition of interest in the future.

Analysis of variance

Analysis of variance is a collection of statistical models used to analyze the differences between group means and their associated procedures (such as 'variation' among and between groups). In ANOVA setting, the observed variance in a particular variable is partitioned into components attributable to different sources of variation. In its simplest form, ANOVA provides a statistical test of whether or not the means of several groups are equal, and therefore generalizes t-test to more than two groups.

Matching

In the mathematical discipline of graph theory, a matching or independent edge set in a graph is a set of edges without common vertices. It may also be an entire graph consisting of edges without common vertices.

Given a graph G = (V,E), a matching M in G is a set of pairwise non-adjacent edges; that is, no two edges share a common vertex.

Multiple regression	In statistics, linear regression is an approach to modeling the relationship between a scalar dependent variable y and one or more explanatory variables denoted X. The case of one explanatory variable is called simple regression. More than one explanatory variable is multiple regression. (This in turn should be distinguished from multivariate linear regression, where multiple correlated dependent variables are predicted, rather than a single scalar variable).
Interaction	In statistics, an interaction may arise when considering the relationship among three or more variables, and describes a situation in which the simultaneous influence of two variables on a third is not additive. Most commonly, interactions are considered in the context of regression analyses. The presence of interactions can have important implications for the interpretation of statistical models.
Paradigm	In the behavioural sciences, e.g. Psychology, Biology, Neurosciences, an experimental paradigm is an experimental setup (i.e. a way to conduct a certain type of experiment) that is defined by certain fine-tuned standards and often has a theoretical background. A paradigm in this technical sense, however, is not a way of thinking as it is in the epistemological meaning. See also: Paradigm, Design of experiments
Variance	In probability theory and statistics, the variance is a measure of how far a set of numbers is spread out. It is one of several descriptors of a probability distribution, describing how far the numbers lie from the mean (expected value). In particular, the variance is one of the moments of a distribution.
Constructivism	In the philosophy of mathematics, constructivism asserts that it is necessary to find a mathematical object to prove that it exists. When one assumes that an object does not exist and derives a contradiction from that assumption, one still has not found the object and therefore not proved its existence, according to constructivism. This viewpoint involves a verificational interpretation of the existence quantifier, which is at odds with its classical interpretation.
Social constructivism	Social constructivism is a sociological theory of knowledge that applies the general philosophical constructivism into social settings, wherein groups construct knowledge for one another, collaboratively creating a small culture of shared artifacts with shared meanings. When one is immersed within a culture of this sort, one is learning all the time about how to be a part of that culture on many levels. Its origins are largely attributed to Lev Vygotsky.
Methodology	Methodology is the systematic, theoretical analysis of the methods applied to a field of study, or the theoretical analysis of the body of methods and principles associated with a branch of knowledge. It, typically, encompasses concepts such as paradigm, theoretical model, phases and quantitative or qualitative techniques.

Phenomenology	The term phenomenology in science is used to describe a body of knowledge that relates empirical observations of phenomena to each other, in a way that is consistent with fundamental theory, but is not directly derived from theory. For example, we find the following definition in the Concise Dictionary of Physics:' Phenomenological Theory. A theory that expresses mathematically the results of observed phenomena without paying detailed attention to their fundamental significance.'
Coding	Coding refers to an analytical process in which data, in both quantitative form (such as questionnaires results) or qualitative (such as interview transcripts) are categorised to facilitate analysis. Coding means the transformation of data into a form understandable by computer software. The classification of information is an important step in preparation of data for computer processing with statistical software.
Heuristic	In computer science and optimization a heuristic is a rule of thumb learned from experience but not always justified by an underlying theory. Heuristics are often used to improve efficiency or effectiveness of optimization algorithms, either by finding an approximate answer when the optimal answer would be prohibitively difficult or to make an algorithm faster. Usually, heuristics do not guarantee that an optimal solution is ever found.
Emic	Emic and etic are terms used by anthropologists and by others in the social and behavioral sciences to refer to two kinds of data concerning human behavior. In particular, they are used in cultural anthropology to refer to kinds of fieldwork done and viewpoints obtained. "".
Grounded theory	Grounded theory method (GT) is a systematic methodology in the social sciences involving the discovery of theory through the analysis of data. It is mainly used in qualitative research, but is also applicable to quantitative data. Grounded theory method is a research method, which operates almost in a reverse fashion from traditional research and at first sight may appear to be in contradiction to the scientific method.
Perspective	Perspective in pharmacoeconomics refers to the economic vantage point that is being taken in a pharmacoeconomic analysis, such as a cost-effectiveness analysis or cost-utility analysis. This will affect the types of costs (resource expenditures) and benefits that will be considered relevant to the analysis. Five general perspectives that are often cited in pharmacoeconomics include: institutional, third party, patient, governmental and societal.
Narrative inquiry	Narrative Inquiry emerged as a discipline within the broader field of qualitative research.

It is an approach to understanding/researching the way people make meaning of their lives as narratives, linked fields are narrative analysis, narratology and life writing. Narrative Inquiry should be distinguished from storytelling in that the word narrative implies an audience and a narrator.

Qualitative Research — Qualitative Research is a bimonthly peer-reviewed academic journal published by SAGE Publications, focusing on qualitative research methods in social sciences and cultural studies. It publishes research articles and review articles.

Action research — Action research is a reflective process of progressive problem solving led by individuals working with others in teams or as part of a 'community of practice' to improve the way they address issues and solve problems. Action research involves the process of actively participating in an organization change situation whilst conducting research. Action research can also be undertaken by larger organizations or institutions, assisted or guided by professional researchers, with the aim of improving their strategies, practices, and knowledge of the environments within which they practice.

Single-subject design — Single-subject design is a research design most often used in applied fields of psychology, education, and human behavior in which the subject serves as his/her own control, rather than using another individual/group. Researchers use single-subject design because these designs are sensitive to individual organism differences vs group designs which are sensitive to averages of groups. Often there will be large numbers of subjects in a research study using single-subject design, however--because the subject serves as their own control, this is still a single-subject design.

Data collection — Data collection is any process of preparing and collecting data, for example, as part of a process improvement or similar project. The purpose of data collection is to obtain information to keep on record, to make decisions about important issues, or to pass information on to others. Data are primarily collected to provide information regarding a specific topic.

Mixed model — A mixed model is a statistical model containing both fixed effects and random effects, that is mixed effects. These models are useful in a wide variety of disciplines in the physical, biological and social sciences. They are particularly useful in settings where repeated measurements are made on the same statistical units, or where measurements are made on clusters of related statistical units.

Collection — In computer science, a collection is a grouping of some variable number of data items (possibly zero) that have some shared significance to the problem being solved and need to be operated upon together in some controlled fashion. Generally, the data items will be of the same type or, in languages supporting inheritance, derived from some common ancestor type. A table is usually not considered a collection because it holds a fixed number of items, although tables/arrays commonly play a role in the implementation of collections.

Statement

In logic a statement is either (a) a meaningful declarative sentence that is either true or false, or (b) what is asserted or made by the use of a declarative sentence. In the latter case, a statement is distinct from a sentence in that a sentence is only one formulation of a statement, whereas there may be many other formulations expressing the same statement.

Philosopher of language, Peter Strawson advocated the use of the term 'statement' in sense (b) in preference to proposition.

Constructionism

Constructionist learning is inspired by the constructivist theory that individual learners construct mental models to understand the world around them. However, constructionism holds that learning can happen most effectively when people are also active in making tangible objects in the real world. In this sense, constructionism is connected with experiential learning, and builds on Jean Piaget's epistemological theory of constructivism..

Process theory

Process theory is a commonly used form of scientific research study in which events or occurrences are said to be the result of certain input states leading to a certain outcome (output) state, following a set process.

Process theory holds that if an outcome is to be duplicated, so too must the process which originally created it, and that there are certain constant necessary conditions for the outcome to be reached. When the phrase is used in connection with human motivation, process theory attempts to explain the mechanism by which human needs changes.

Meta-analysis

In statistics, a meta-analysis refers to methods focused on contrasting and combining results from different studies, in the hope of identifying patterns among study results, sources of disagreement among those results, or other interesting relationships that may come to light in the context of multiple studies. In its simplest form, this is normally by identification of a common measure of effect size, of which a weighted average might be the output of a meta-analysis. The weighting might be related to sample sizes within the individual studies.

3. Methods of Inquiry: Quantitative and Qualitative Approaches

CHAPTER QUIZ: KEY TERMS, PEOPLE, PLACES, CONCEPTS

1. _________, logical empiricism, or neopositivism embraced verificationism, a set of theories of knowledge that combined logicism, empiricism, and linguistics to ground philosophy on a basis consistent with exemplary examples of empirical sciences. Seeking to overhaul all of philosophy and convert it to a new scientific philosophy, the movement emerged in the late 1920s from the Berlin Circle and from the Vienna Circle.

   Appalled by Western society's flaring racism, bigotry, and nationalism, but perhaps no less by countermovements toward metaphysics, mysticism, and intuition, logical positivists were inspired by developments in mathematical logic, philosophy of language, and physics, especially general theory of relativity.

   a. Logical positivism
   b. Research fellow
   c. Research Fortnight
   d. Research proposal

2. The _________, first so-named by William Whewell, is a proposed description of scientific method. According to it, scientific inquiry proceeds by formulating a hypothesis in a form that could conceivably be falsified by a test on observable data. A test that could and does run contrary to predictions of the hypothesis is taken as a falsification of the hypothesis.

   a. Hypothetico-deductive model
   b. Law
   c. Medawar Lecture
   d. Mediocrity principle

3. In probability theory and statistics, the _________ is a measure of how far a set of numbers is spread out. It is one of several descriptors of a probability distribution, describing how far the numbers lie from the mean (expected value). In particular, the _________ is one of the moments of a distribution.

   a. Variation ratio
   b. Variogram
   c. Provocation test
   d. Variance

4. . _________ is the branch of philosophy concerned with the nature and scope of knowledge and is also referred to as 'theory of knowledge'. It questions what knowledge is and how it can be acquired, and the extent to which any given subject or entity can be known.

   Much of the debate in this field has focused on analyzing the nature of knowledge and how it relates to connected notions such as truth, belief, and justification.

   a. Epistemology
   b. International Geosphere-Biosphere Programme
   c. A. Edward Nussbaum

5. _________ is a theory of knowledge that asserts that knowledge comes only or primarily from sensory experience. One of several views of epistemology, the study of human knowledge, along with rationalism, idealism, and historicism, _________ emphasizes the role of experience and evidence, especially sensory perception, in the formation of ideas, over the notion of innate ideas or traditions; empiricists may argue however that traditions arise due to relations of previous sense experiences.

_________ in the philosophy of science emphasizes evidence, especially as discovered in experiments.

a. Empiricism
b. American Association for Public Opinion Research
c. International Geosphere-Biosphere Programme
d. Error bar

ANSWER KEY

3. Methods of Inquiry: Quantitative and Qualitative Approaches

1. a
2. a
3. d
4. a
5. a

4. Literature Review and Statement of the Problem

CHAPTER OUTLINE: KEY TERMS, PEOPLE, PLACES, CONCEPTS

- Argument
- Research design
- Case studies
- Variable
- Venn diagram
- Hypothetico-deductive model
- Statement
- Content
- Operationalization
- Research question
- Brainstorming
- Narrative inquiry
- Action research
- APA style
- Publication Manual of the American Psychological Association

4. Literature Review and Statement of the Problem

CHAPTER HIGHLIGHTS & NOTES: KEY TERMS, PEOPLE, PLACES, CONCEPTS

Argument	In logic and philosophy, an argument is an attempt to persuade someone of something, by giving reasons for accepting a particular conclusion as evident. The general structure of an argument in a natural language is that of premises (typically in the form of propositions, statements or sentences) in support of a claim: the conclusion. The structure of some arguments can also be set out in a formal language, and formally-defined 'arguments' can be made independently of natural language arguments, as in math, logic and computer science.
Research design	Research design is considered as a 'blueprint' for research, dealing with at least four problems: which questions to study, which data are relevant, what data to collect, and how to analyze the results.. The best design depends on the research question as well as the orientation of the researcher. Every design has its positive and negative sides.
Case studies	In the social sciences and life sciences, a case study is a descriptive or explanatory analysis of a person, group or event. An explanatory case study is used to explore causation in order to find underlying principles. Case studies may be prospective (in which criteria are established and cases fitting the criteria are included as they become available) or retrospective (in which criteria are established for selecting cases from historical records for inclusion in the study).
Variable	In mathematics, a variable is a value that may change within the scope of a given problem or set of operations. In contrast, a constant is a value that remains unchanged, though often unknown or undetermined. The concepts of constants and variables are fundamental to many areas of mathematics and its applications.
Venn diagram	Venn diagrams or set diagrams are diagrams that show all possible logical relations between a finite collection of sets (aggregation of things). Venn diagrams were conceived around 1880 by John Venn. They are used to teach elementary set theory, as well as illustrate simple set relationships in probability, logic, statistics, linguistics and computer science .
Hypothetico-deductive model	The hypothetico-deductive model, first so-named by William Whewell, is a proposed description of scientific method. According to it, scientific inquiry proceeds by formulating a hypothesis in a form that could conceivably be falsified by a test on observable data. A test that could and does run contrary to predictions of the hypothesis is taken as a falsification of the hypothesis.
Statement	In logic a statement is either (a) a meaningful declarative sentence that is either true or false, or (b) what is asserted or made by the use of a declarative sentence. In the latter case, a statement is distinct from a sentence in that a sentence is only one formulation of a statement, whereas there may be many other formulations expressing the same statement. Philosopher of language, Peter Strawson advocated the use of the term 'statement' in sense (b) in preference to proposition.
Content	In algebra, the content of a polynomial is the highest common factor of its coefficients.

A polynomial is primitive if it has content unity.

Gauss's lemma for polynomials may be expressed as stating that for polynomials over a unique factorization domain, the content of the product of two polynomials is the product of their contents.

Operationalization

Operationalization is the process of defining a fuzzy concept so as to make the concept clearly distinguishable (in humanities) or measurable (in physicalist sciences) and to understand it in terms of empirical observations. In a wider sense it refers to the process of specifying the extension of a concept - in other words, describing what is and is not a part of that concept.

Operationalization often means creating operational definitions and theoretical definitions.

Research question

A research question is the methodological point of departure of scholarly research in both the natural sciences and humanities. The research will answer any question posed. At an undergraduate level, the answer to the research question is the thesis statement.

Brainstorming

Brainstorming is a group or individual creativity technique by which efforts are made to find a conclusion for a specific problem by gathering a list of ideas spontaneously contributed by its member. The term was popularized by Alex Faickney Osborn in the 1953 book Applied Imagination. Osborn claimed that brainstorming was more effective than individuals working alone in generating ideas, although more recent research has questioned this conclusion. Today, the term is used as a catch all for all group ideation sessions.

Narrative inquiry

Narrative Inquiry emerged as a discipline within the broader field of qualitative research. It is an approach to understanding/researching the way people make meaning of their lives as narratives, linked fields are narrative analysis, narratology and life writing. Narrative Inquiry should be distinguished from storytelling in that the word narrative implies an audience and a narrator.

Action research

Action research is a reflective process of progressive problem solving led by individuals working with others in teams or as part of a 'community of practice' to improve the way they address issues and solve problems. Action research involves the process of actively participating in an organization change situation whilst conducting research. Action research can also be undertaken by larger organizations or institutions, assisted or guided by professional researchers, with the aim of improving their strategies, practices, and knowledge of the environments within which they practice.

APA style

American Psychological Association style is an academic format specified in The Publication Manual of the American Psychological Association, a style guide that offers academic authors guidance on various subjects for the submission of papers to the publications of APA.

4. Literature Review and Statement of the Problem

CHAPTER HIGHLIGHTS & NOTES: KEY TERMS, PEOPLE, PLACES, CONCEPTS

	The APA states that the guidelines were developed to assist reading comprehension in the social and behavioral sciences, for clarity of communication, and for 'word choice that best reduces bias in language'. The Publication Manual of the American Psychological Association contains guidelines on many aspects of academic writing as it is seen appropriate by the APA. Among the topics covered are information on the structure of research papers of various kinds, spelling rules, an author-date reference style, construction of tables and graphs, plagiarism, formatting of papers, and much more. APA style is widely used, not only by APA publications but by various other scientific journals (including medical and public health journals), textbooks, and academia (for papers written in classes).
Publication Manual of the American Psychological Association	American Psychological Association style is an academic format specified in The Publication Manual of the American Psychological Association, a style guide that offers academic authors guidance on various subjects for the submission of papers to the publications of APA. The APA states that the guidelines were developed to assist reading comprehension in the social and behavioral sciences, for clarity of communication, and for 'word choice that best reduces bias in language'. The Publication Manual of the American Psychological Association contains guidelines on many aspects of academic writing as it is seen appropriate by the APA. Among the topics covered are information on the structure of research papers of various kinds, spelling rules, an author-date reference style, construction of tables and graphs, plagiarism, formatting of papers, and much more.

CHAPTER QUIZ: KEY TERMS, PEOPLE, PLACES, CONCEPTS

1. _________ emerged as a discipline within the broader field of qualitative research. It is an approach to understanding/researching the way people make meaning of their lives as narratives, linked fields are narrative analysis, narratology and life writing. _________ should be distinguished from storytelling in that the word narrative implies an audience and a narrator.

   a. Naturalistic observation
   b. Participant observation
   c. Narrative inquiry
   d. Provalis Research

2. . The _________, first so-named by William Whewell, is a proposed description of scientific method. According to it, scientific inquiry proceeds by formulating a hypothesis in a form that could conceivably be falsified by a test on observable data. A test that could and does run contrary to predictions of the hypothesis is taken as a falsification of the hypothesis.

   a. Lakatos Award
   b. Hypothetico-deductive model

c. Medawar Lecture
d. Mediocrity principle

3. _________ is the process of defining a fuzzy concept so as to make the concept clearly distinguishable (in humanities) or measurable (in physicalist sciences) and to understand it in terms of empirical observations. In a wider sense it refers to the process of specifying the extension of a concept - in other words, describing what is and is not a part of that concept.

_________ often means creating operational definitions and theoretical definitions.

a. Adversarial review
b. Operationalization
c. Empirical method
d. Evidence-based practice

4. In logic and philosophy, an _________ is an attempt to persuade someone of something, by giving reasons for accepting a particular conclusion as evident. The general structure of an _________ in a natural language is that of premises (typically in the form of propositions, statements or sentences) in support of a claim: the conclusion. The structure of some _________s can also be set out in a formal language, and formally-defined '_________s' can be made independently of natural language _________s, as in math, logic and computer science.

a. Argument
b. Cauchy's integral theorem
c. Complex analytic geometry
d. Conformal welding

5. American Psychological Association style is an academic format specified in The Publication Manual of the American Psychological Association, a style guide that offers academic authors guidance on various subjects for the submission of papers to the publications of APA. The APA states that the guidelines were developed to assist reading comprehension in the social and behavioral sciences, for clarity of communication, and for 'word choice that best reduces bias in language'. The Publication Manual of the American Psychological Association contains guidelines on many aspects of academic writing as it is seen appropriate by the APA. Among the topics covered are information on the structure of research papers of various kinds, spelling rules, an author-date reference style, construction of tables and graphs, plagiarism, formatting of papers, and much more.

_________ is widely used, not only by APA publications but by various other scientific journals (including medical and public health journals), textbooks, and academia (for papers written in classes).

a. APA style
b. Artificial society
c. Experimental research design
d. Impact evaluation

ANSWER KEY
4. Literature Review and Statement of the Problem

---

1. c
2. b
3. b
4. a
5. a

---

5. The Method Chapter : Describing Your Research Plan

CHAPTER OUTLINE: KEY TERMS, PEOPLE, PLACES, CONCEPTS

- Hypothetico-deductive model
- Research design
- Case studies
- Data analysis
- Design statement
- Statement
- Sampling
- Sampling design
- Data collection
- Collection
- Recruitment
- Sample size
- Variable
- Interaction
- Census
- Reliability
- Validity
- Development
- Demographic
- Inferential statistics
- Moderator variable

CHAPTER OUTLINE: KEY TERMS, PEOPLE, PLACES, CONCEPTS

______	Phenomenology
______	Coding
______	Grounded theory
______	Observational study
______	Internal validity
______	Audit trail
______	Member check
______	Triangulation
______	Peer review

CHAPTER HIGHLIGHTS & NOTES: KEY TERMS, PEOPLE, PLACES, CONCEPTS

Hypothetico-deductive model	The hypothetico-deductive model, first so-named by William Whewell, is a proposed description of scientific method. According to it, scientific inquiry proceeds by formulating a hypothesis in a form that could conceivably be falsified by a test on observable data. A test that could and does run contrary to predictions of the hypothesis is taken as a falsification of the hypothesis.
Research design	Research design is considered as a 'blueprint' for research, dealing with at least four problems: which questions to study, which data are relevant, what data to collect, and how to analyze the results.. The best design depends on the research question as well as the orientation of the researcher. Every design has its positive and negative sides.
Case studies	In the social sciences and life sciences, a case study is a descriptive or explanatory analysis of a person, group or event. An explanatory case study is used to explore causation in order to find underlying principles. Case studies may be prospective (in which criteria are established and cases fitting the criteria are included as they become available) or retrospective (in which criteria are established for selecting cases from historical records for inclusion in the study).

5. The Method Chapter : Describing Your Research Plan

CHAPTER HIGHLIGHTS & NOTES: KEY TERMS, PEOPLE, PLACES, CONCEPTS

Data analysis

Analysis of data is a process of inspecting, cleaning, transforming, and modeling data with the goal of highlighting useful information, suggesting conclusions, and supporting decision making. Data analysis has multiple facets and approaches, encompassing diverse techniques under a variety of names, in different business, science, and social science domains.

Data mining is a particular data analysis technique that focuses on modeling and knowledge discovery for predictive rather than purely descriptive purposes.

Design statement

A design statement is a report required under English and Welsh planning law that sets out, illustrates and justifies the process that has led to the development proposals. It is required to be submitted to accompany a planning application.

The DCLG circular 01/2006 and the Planning and Compulsory Purchase Act 2004, compulsorily requires applicants to provide a Design & Access Statement as part of any planning application from the 10th August 2006. This includes outline planning applications.

Statement

In logic a statement is either (a) a meaningful declarative sentence that is either true or false, or (b) what is asserted or made by the use of a declarative sentence. In the latter case, a statement is distinct from a sentence in that a sentence is only one formulation of a statement, whereas there may be many other formulations expressing the same statement.

Philosopher of language, Peter Strawson advocated the use of the term 'statement' in sense (b) in preference to proposition.

Sampling

In statistics and survey methodology, sampling is concerned with the selection of a subset of individuals from within a population to estimate characteristics of the whole population.

Researchers rarely survey the entire population because the cost of a census is too high. The three main advantages of sampling are that the cost is lower, data collection is faster, and since the data set is smaller it is possible to ensure homogeneity and to improve the accuracy and quality of the data.

Sampling design

In the theory of finite population sampling, a sampling design specifies for every possible sample its probability of being drawn.

Mathematically, a sampling design is denoted by the function $P(S)$ which gives the probability of drawing a sample S.

Data collection

Data collection is any process of preparing and collecting data, for example, as part of a process improvement or similar project. The purpose of data collection is to obtain information to keep on record, to make decisions about important issues, or to pass information on to others.

Collection

In computer science, a collection is a grouping of some variable number of data items (possibly zero) that have some shared significance to the problem being solved and need to be operated upon together in some controlled fashion. Generally, the data items will be of the same type or, in languages supporting inheritance, derived from some common ancestor type. A table is usually not considered a collection because it holds a fixed number of items, although tables/arrays commonly play a role in the implementation of collections.

Recruitment

Recruitment refers to the process of attracting, screening, selecting, and onboarding a qualified person for a job. At the strategic level it may involve the development of an employer brand which includes an 'employee offering'.

The stages of the recruitment process include: job analysis and developing a person specification; the sourcing of candidates by networking, advertising, or other search methods; matching candidates to job requirements and screening individuals using testing (skills or personality assessment); assessment of candidates' motivations and their fit with organizational requirements by interviewing and other assessment techniques.

Sample size

Sample size determination is the act of choosing the number of observations or replicates to include in a statistical sample. The sample size is an important feature of any empirical study in which the goal is to make inferences about a population from a sample. In practice, the sample size used in a study is determined based on the expense of data collection, and the need to have sufficient statistical power.

Variable

In mathematics, a variable is a value that may change within the scope of a given problem or set of operations. In contrast, a constant is a value that remains unchanged, though often unknown or undetermined. The concepts of constants and variables are fundamental to many areas of mathematics and its applications.

Interaction

In statistics, an interaction may arise when considering the relationship among three or more variables, and describes a situation in which the simultaneous influence of two variables on a third is not additive. Most commonly, interactions are considered in the context of regression analyses.

The presence of interactions can have important implications for the interpretation of statistical models.

Census

A census is the procedure of systematically acquiring and recording information about the members of a given population. It is a regularly occurring and official count of a particular population. The term is used mostly in connection with national population and housing censuses; other common censuses include agriculture, business, and traffic censuses.

Reliability

In statistics, reliability refers to the consistency of a measure. A measure is said to have a high reliability if it produces consistent results under consistent conditions.

5. The Method Chapter : Describing Your Research Plan

Validity	In science and statistics, validity has no single agreed definition but generally refers to the extent to which a concept, conclusion or measurement is well-founded and corresponds accurately to the real world. The word 'valid' is derived from the Latin validus, meaning strong. The validity of a measurement tool (for example, a test in education) is considered to be the degree to which the tool measures what it claims to measure.
Development	In classical differential geometry, development refers to the simple idea of rolling one smooth surface over another in Euclidean space. For example, the tangent plane to a surface (such as the sphere or the cylinder) at a point can be rolled around the surface to obtain the tangent-plane at other points. The tangential contact between the surfaces being rolled over one another provides a relation between points on the two surfaces.
Demographic	Demographics are statistical characteristics of a population. These types of data are used widely in public opinion polling and marketing. Commonly examined demographics include gender, age, ethnicity, knowledge of languages, disabilities, mobility, home ownership, employment status, and even location.
Inferential statistics	In statistics, statistical inference is the process of drawing conclusions from data that is subject to random variation, for example, observational errors or sampling variation. More substantially, the terms statistical inference, statistical induction and inferential statistics are used to describe systems of procedures that can be used to draw conclusions from datasets arising from systems affected by random variation, such as observational errors, random sampling, or random experimentation. Initial requirements of such a system of procedures for inference and induction are that the system should produce reasonable answers when applied to well-defined situations and that it should be general enough to be applied across a range of situations.
Moderator variable	In statistics and regression analysis, moderation occurs when the relationship between two variables depends on a third variable. The third variable is referred to as the moderator variable or simply the moderator. The effect of a moderating variable is characterized statistically as an interaction; that is, a qualitative (e.g., sex, race, class) or quantitative (e.g., level of reward) variable that affects the direction and/or strength of the relation between dependent and independent variables.
Phenomenology	The term phenomenology in science is used to describe a body of knowledge that relates empirical observations of phenomena to each other, in a way that is consistent with fundamental theory, but is not directly derived from theory. For example, we find the following definition in the Concise Dictionary of Physics:' Phenomenological Theory.

Coding	Coding refers to an analytical process in which data, in both quantitative form (such as questionnaires results) or qualitative (such as interview transcripts) are categorised to facilitate analysis. Coding means the transformation of data into a form understandable by computer software. The classification of information is an important step in preparation of data for computer processing with statistical software.
Grounded theory	Grounded theory method (GT) is a systematic methodology in the social sciences involving the discovery of theory through the analysis of data. It is mainly used in qualitative research, but is also applicable to quantitative data. Grounded theory method is a research method, which operates almost in a reverse fashion from traditional research and at first sight may appear to be in contradiction to the scientific method.
Observational study	In epidemiology and statistics, an observational study draws inferences about the possible effect of a treatment on subjects, where the assignment of subjects into a treated group versus a control group is outside the control of the investigator. This is in contrast with experiments, such as randomized controlled trials, where each subject is randomly assigned to a treated group or a control group. The assignment of treatments may be beyond the control of the investigator for a variety of reasons:•A randomized experiment would violate ethical standards.
Internal validity	Internal validity is a property of scientific studies which reflects the extent to which a causal conclusion based on a study is warranted. Such warrant is constituted by the extent to which a study minimizes systematic error (or 'bias').
Audit trail	An audit trail is a security-relevant chronological record, set of records, or destination and source of records that provide documentary evidence of the sequence of activities that have affected at any time a specific operation, procedure, or event. Audit records typically result from activities such as financial transactions, scientific research and health care data transactions, or communications by individual people, systems, accounts, or other entities. The process that creates an audit trail is typically required to always run in a privileged mode, so it can access and supervise all actions from all users; a normal user should not be allowed to stop/change it.
Member check	In qualitative research, a member check, is a technique used by researchers to help improve the accuracy, credibility, validity, and transferability (also known as applicability, external validity, or fittingness) of a study.. There are many subcategories of members checks, including; narrative accuracy checks, interpretive validity, descriptive validity, theoretical valdity, and evaluative validity.

5. The Method Chapter : Describing Your Research Plan

CHAPTER HIGHLIGHTS & NOTES: KEY TERMS, PEOPLE, PLACES, CONCEPTS

Triangulation

In the social sciences, triangulation is often used to indicate that more than two methods are used in a study with a view to double checking results. This is also called 'cross examination'.

The idea is that one can be more confident with a result if different methods lead to the same result.

Peer review

Peer review is a process of self-regulation by a profession or a process of evaluation involving qualified individuals within the relevant field. Peer review methods are employed to maintain standards, improve performance and provide credibility. In academia peer review is often used to determine an academic paper's suitability for publication.

CHAPTER QUIZ: KEY TERMS, PEOPLE, PLACES, CONCEPTS

1. The _________, first so-named by William Whewell, is a proposed description of scientific method. According to it, scientific inquiry proceeds by formulating a hypothesis in a form that could conceivably be falsified by a test on observable data. A test that could and does run contrary to predictions of the hypothesis is taken as a falsification of the hypothesis.

   a. Lakatos Award
   b. Law
   c. Medawar Lecture
   d. Hypothetico-deductive model

2. In logic a _________ is either (a) a meaningful declarative sentence that is either true or false, or (b) what is asserted or made by the use of a declarative sentence. In the latter case, a _________ is distinct from a sentence in that a sentence is only one formulation of a _________, whereas there may be many other formulations expressing the same _________.

   Philosopher of language, Peter Strawson advocated the use of the term '_________' in sense (b) in preference to proposition.

   a. Term logic
   b. Tetralemma
   c. Train of thought
   d. Statement

3. . _________ refers to an analytical process in which data, in both quantitative form (such as questionnaires results) or qualitative (such as interview transcripts) are categorised to facilitate analysis.

   _________ means the transformation of data into a form understandable by computer software. The classification of information is an important step in preparation of data for computer processing with statistical software.

a. Social network change detection
b. Philosophy of Artificial Intelligence and Cognitive Science
c. Philosophy of chemistry
d. Coding

4. In epidemiology and statistics, an _________ draws inferences about the possible effect of a treatment on subjects, where the assignment of subjects into a treated group versus a control group is outside the control of the investigator. This is in contrast with experiments, such as randomized controlled trials, where each subject is randomly assigned to a treated group or a control group.

   The assignment of treatments may be beyond the control of the investigator for a variety of reasons:•A randomized experiment would violate ethical standards.

   a. Observational study
   b. One-factor-at-a-time method
   c. Open-label trial
   d. Orthogonal array testing

5. _________ is a process of self-regulation by a profession or a process of evaluation involving qualified individuals within the relevant field. _________ methods are employed to maintain standards, improve performance and provide credibility. In academia _________ is often used to determine an academic paper's suitability for publication.

   a. Personoid
   b. Pilot experiment
   c. Peer review
   d. Scientific control

ANSWER KEY

5. The Method Chapter : Describing Your Research Plan

---

1. d
2. d
3. d
4. a
5. c

---

6. Presenting the Results of Quantitative Studies

CHAPTER OUTLINE: KEY TERMS, PEOPLE, PLACES, CONCEPTS

- Coding
- Data analysis
- Exploratory data analysis
- Statement
- Dependence
- Empiricism
- Research question
- Brainstorming
- Probability
- Publication Manual of the American Psychological Association
- APA style
- Authorship
- Mnemonic
- Two-tailed test
- Effect size
- Statistical significance
- Data collection
- Hypothetico-deductive model
- Variable
- Collection
- Multiple regression

6. Presenting the Results of Quantitative Studies

CHAPTER OUTLINE: KEY TERMS, PEOPLE, PLACES, CONCEPTS

- Sample size
- Frequency
- Regression analysis
- Difference
- Deviation
- Standard deviation
- Scatter plot
- Inferential statistics
- Chi-square test
- Analysis of variance
- Variance
- Confidence interval
- Interval
- Multiple correlation

6. Presenting the Results of Quantitative Studies

Coding

Coding refers to an analytical process in which data, in both quantitative form (such as questionnaires results) or qualitative (such as interview transcripts) are categorised to facilitate analysis.

Coding means the transformation of data into a form understandable by computer software. The classification of information is an important step in preparation of data for computer processing with statistical software.

Data analysis

Analysis of data is a process of inspecting, cleaning, transforming, and modeling data with the goal of highlighting useful information, suggesting conclusions, and supporting decision making. Data analysis has multiple facets and approaches, encompassing diverse techniques under a variety of names, in different business, science, and social science domains.

Data mining is a particular data analysis technique that focuses on modeling and knowledge discovery for predictive rather than purely descriptive purposes.

Exploratory data analysis

In statistics, exploratory data analysis is an approach to analyzing data sets to summarize their main characteristics in easy-to-understand form, often with visual graphs, without using a statistical model or having formulated a hypothesis. Exploratory data analysis was promoted by John Tukey to encourage statisticians visually to examine their data sets, to formulate hypotheses that could be tested on new data-sets.

Tukey's championing of EDA encouraged the development of statistical computing packages, especially S at Bell Labs: The S programming language inspired the systems 'S'-PLUS and R. This family of statistical-computing environments featured vastly improved dynamic visualization capabilities, which allowed statisticians to identify outliers and patterns in data that merited further study.

Statement

In logic a statement is either (a) a meaningful declarative sentence that is either true or false, or (b) what is asserted or made by the use of a declarative sentence. In the latter case, a statement is distinct from a sentence in that a sentence is only one formulation of a statement, whereas there may be many other formulations expressing the same statement.

Philosopher of language, Peter Strawson advocated the use of the term 'statement' in sense (b) in preference to proposition.

Dependence

In statistics, dependence refers to any statistical relationship between two random variables or two sets of data. Correlation refers to any of a broad class of statistical relationships involving dependence.

Empiricism	Empiricism is a theory of knowledge that asserts that knowledge comes only or primarily from sensory experience. One of several views of epistemology, the study of human knowledge, along with rationalism, idealism, and historicism, empiricism emphasizes the role of experience and evidence, especially sensory perception, in the formation of ideas, over the notion of innate ideas or traditions; empiricists may argue however that traditions arise due to relations of previous sense experiences. Empiricism in the philosophy of science emphasizes evidence, especially as discovered in experiments.
Research question	A research question is the methodological point of departure of scholarly research in both the natural sciences and humanities. The research will answer any question posed. At an undergraduate level, the answer to the research question is the thesis statement.
Brainstorming	Brainstorming is a group or individual creativity technique by which efforts are made to find a conclusion for a specific problem by gathering a list of ideas spontaneously contributed by its member. The term was popularized by Alex Faickney Osborn in the 1953 book Applied Imagination. Osborn claimed that brainstorming was more effective than individuals working alone in generating ideas, although more recent research has questioned this conclusion. Today, the term is used as a catch all for all group ideation sessions.
Probability	Probability is a measure or estimation of how likely it is that something will happen or that a statement is true. Probabilities are given a value between 0 (0% chance or will not happen) and 1 (100% chance or will happen). The higher the degree of probability, the more likely the event is to happen, or, in a longer series of samples, the greater the number of times such event is expected to happen.
Publication Manual of the American Psychological Association	American Psychological Association style is an academic format specified in The Publication Manual of the American Psychological Association, a style guide that offers academic authors guidance on various subjects for the submission of papers to the publications of APA. The APA states that the guidelines were developed to assist reading comprehension in the social and behavioral sciences, for clarity of communication, and for 'word choice that best reduces bias in language'. The Publication Manual of the American Psychological Association contains guidelines on many aspects of academic writing as it is seen appropriate by the APA. Among the topics covered are information on the structure of research papers of various kinds, spelling rules, an author-date reference style, construction of tables and graphs, plagiarism, formatting of papers, and much more.
APA style	American Psychological Association style is an academic format specified in The Publication Manual of the American Psychological Association, a style guide that offers academic authors guidance on various subjects for the submission of papers to the publications of APA.

The APA states that the guidelines were developed to assist reading comprehension in the social and behavioral sciences, for clarity of communication, and for 'word choice that best reduces bias in language'. The Publication Manual of the American Psychological Association contains guidelines on many aspects of academic writing as it is seen appropriate by the APA. Among the topics covered are information on the structure of research papers of various kinds, spelling rules, an author-date reference style, construction of tables and graphs, plagiarism, formatting of papers, and much more.

APA style is widely used, not only by APA publications but by various other scientific journals (including medical and public health journals), textbooks, and academia (for papers written in classes).

Authorship

An author is broadly defined as 'the person who originated or gave existence to anything' and whose authorship determines responsibility for what was created. Narrowly defined, an author is the originator of any written work.

Mnemonic

A mnemonic, is any learning technique that aids information retention. Mnemonics aim to translate information into a form that the human brain can retain better than its original form. Even the process of applying this conversion might already aid the transfer of information to long-term memory.

Two-tailed test

In statistical significance testing, a one-tailed test or two-tailed test are alternative ways of computing the statistical significance of a data set in terms of a test statistic, depending on whether only one direction is considered extreme or both directions are considered extreme. Alternative names are one-sided and two-sided tests; the terminology 'tail' is because the extremes of distributions are often small, as in the normal distribution or 'bell curve', pictured above right.

If the test statistic is always positive (or zero), only the one-tailed test is generally applicable, while if the test statistic can assume positive and negative values, both the one-tailed and two-tailed test are of use.

Effect size

In statistics, an effect size is a measure of the strength of the relationship between two variables in a statistical population, or a sample-based estimate of that quantity. An effect size calculated from data is a descriptive statistic that conveys the estimated magnitude of a relationship without making any statement about whether the apparent relationship in the data reflects a true relationship in the population. In that way, effect sizes complement inferential statistics such as p-values.

Statistical significance

Statistical significance is a statistical assessment of whether observations reflect a pattern rather than just chance. The fundamental challenge is that any partial picture of a given hypothesis, poll or question is subject to random error.

Data collection

Data collection is any process of preparing and collecting data, for example, as part of a process improvement or similar project. The purpose of data collection is to obtain information to keep on record, to make decisions about important issues, or to pass information on to others. Data are primarily collected to provide information regarding a specific topic.

Hypothetico-deductive model

The hypothetico-deductive model, first so-named by William Whewell, is a proposed description of scientific method. According to it, scientific inquiry proceeds by formulating a hypothesis in a form that could conceivably be falsified by a test on observable data. A test that could and does run contrary to predictions of the hypothesis is taken as a falsification of the hypothesis.

Variable

In mathematics, a variable is a value that may change within the scope of a given problem or set of operations. In contrast, a constant is a value that remains unchanged, though often unknown or undetermined. The concepts of constants and variables are fundamental to many areas of mathematics and its applications.

Collection

In computer science, a collection is a grouping of some variable number of data items (possibly zero) that have some shared significance to the problem being solved and need to be operated upon together in some controlled fashion. Generally, the data items will be of the same type or, in languages supporting inheritance, derived from some common ancestor type. A table is usually not considered a collection because it holds a fixed number of items, although tables/arrays commonly play a role in the implementation of collections.

Multiple regression

In statistics, linear regression is an approach to modeling the relationship between a scalar dependent variable y and one or more explanatory variables denoted X. The case of one explanatory variable is called simple regression. More than one explanatory variable is multiple regression. (This in turn should be distinguished from multivariate linear regression, where multiple correlated dependent variables are predicted, rather than a single scalar variable).

Sample size

Sample size determination is the act of choosing the number of observations or replicates to include in a statistical sample. The sample size is an important feature of any empirical study in which the goal is to make inferences about a population from a sample. In practice, the sample size used in a study is determined based on the expense of data collection, and the need to have sufficient statistical power.

Frequency

In statistics the frequency of an event i is the number n_i of times the event occurred in the experiment or the study. These frequencies are often graphically represented in histograms.

We speak of absolute frequencies, when the counts n_i themselves are given and of (relative) frequencies, when those are normalized by the total number of events: $f_i = \frac{n_i}{N} = \frac{n_i}{\sum_i n_i}.$

6. Presenting the Results of Quantitative Studies

CHAPTER HIGHLIGHTS & NOTES: KEY TERMS, PEOPLE, PLACES, CONCEPTS

Regression analysis	In statistics, regression analysis includes many techniques for modeling and analyzing several variables, when the focus is on the relationship between a dependent variable and one or more independent variables. More specifically, regression analysis helps one understand how the typical value of the dependent variable changes when any one of the independent variables is varied, while the other independent variables are held fixed. Most commonly, regression analysis estimates the conditional expectation of the dependent variable given the independent variables -- that is, the average value of the dependent variable when the independent variables are held fixed.
Difference	Difference is a key concept of continental philosophy, denoting the process or set of properties by which one entity is distinguished from another within a relational field or a given conceptual system. In the Western philosophical system, difference is traditionally viewed as being opposed to identity, following the Principles of Leibniz, and in particular his Law of the Identity of indiscernibles. In structuralist and poststructuralist accounts, however, difference is understood to be constitutive of both meaning and identity.
Deviation	In mathematics and statistics, deviation is a measure of difference between the observed value and the mean. The sign of deviation (positive or negative), reports the direction of that difference (it is larger when the sign is positive, and smaller if it is negative). The magnitude of the value indicates the size of the difference.
Standard deviation	In statistics and probability theory, standard deviation shows how much variation or dispersion exists from the average (mean), or expected value. A low standard deviation indicates that the data points tend to be very close to the mean; high standard deviation indicates that the data points are spread out over a large range of values. The standard deviation of a random variable, statistical population, data set, or probability distribution is the square root of its variance.
Scatter plot	A scatter plot is a type of mathematical diagram using Cartesian coordinates to display values for two variables for a set of data. The data is displayed as a collection of points, each having the value of one variable determining the position on the horizontal axis and the value of the other variable determining the position on the vertical axis. This kind of plot is also called a scatter chart, scattergram, scatter diagram or scatter graph.
Inferential statistics	In statistics, statistical inference is the process of drawing conclusions from data that is subject to random variation, for example, observational errors or sampling variation. More substantially, the terms statistical inference, statistical induction and inferential statistics are used to describe systems of procedures that can be used to draw conclusions from datasets arising from systems affected by random variation, such as observational errors, random sampling, or random experimentation.

Chi-square test

A chi-square test is any statistical hypothesis test in which the sampling distribution of the test statistic is a chi-square distribution when the null hypothesis is true, or any in which this is asymptotically true, meaning that the sampling distribution (if the null hypothesis is true) can be made to approximate a chi-square distribution as closely as desired by making the sample size large enough.

Some examples of chi-squared tests where the chi-square distribution is only approximately valid:•Pearson's chi-square test, also known as the chi-square goodness-of-fit test or chi-square test for independence. When mentioned without any modifiers or without other precluding context, this test is usually understood .•Yates' chi-square test, also known as Yates' correction for continuity•Cochran-Mantel-Haenszel chi-square test.•Linear-by-linear association chi-square test.•The portmanteau test in time-series analysis, testing for the presence of autocorrelation•Likelihood-ratio tests in general statistical modelling, for testing whether there is evidence of the need to move from a simple model to a more complicated one (where the simple model is nested within the complicated one).

One case where the distribution of the test statistic is an exact chi-square distribution is the test that the variance of a normally-distributed population has a given value based on a sample variance.

Analysis of variance

Analysis of variance is a collection of statistical models used to analyze the differences between group means and their associated procedures (such as 'variation' among and between groups). In ANOVA setting, the observed variance in a particular variable is partitioned into components attributable to different sources of variation. In its simplest form, ANOVA provides a statistical test of whether or not the means of several groups are equal, and therefore generalizes t-test to more than two groups.

Variance

In probability theory and statistics, the variance is a measure of how far a set of numbers is spread out. It is one of several descriptors of a probability distribution, describing how far the numbers lie from the mean (expected value). In particular, the variance is one of the moments of a distribution.

Confidence interval

In statistics, a confidence interval is a kind of interval estimate of a population parameter and is used to indicate the reliability of an estimate. It is an observed interval (i.e. it is calculated from the observations), in principle different from sample to sample, that frequently includes the parameter of interest, if the experiment is repeated. How frequently the observed interval contains the parameter is determined by the confidence level or confidence coefficient.

Interval

In mathematics, a (real) interval is a set of real numbers with the property that any number that lies between two numbers in the set is also included in the set. For example, the set of all numbers x satisfying $0 \leq x \leq 1$ is an interval which contains 0 and 1, as well as all numbers between them. Other examples of intervals are the set of all real numbers

6. Presenting the Results of Quantitative Studies

CHAPTER HIGHLIGHTS & NOTES: KEY TERMS, PEOPLE, PLACES, CONCEPTS

Multiple correlation	In statistics, multiple correlation is a linear relationship among more than two variables. It is measured by the coefficient of multiple determination, denoted as R^2, which is a measure of the fit of a linear regression. A regression's R^2 falls somewhere between zero and one (assuming a constant term has been included in the regression); a higher value indicates a stronger relationship among the variables, with a value of one indicating that all data points fall exactly on a line in multidimensional space and a value of zero indicating no relationship at all between the independent variables collectively and the dependent variable.

CHAPTER QUIZ: KEY TERMS, PEOPLE, PLACES, CONCEPTS

1. _________ determination is the act of choosing the number of observations or replicates to include in a statistical sample. The _________ is an important feature of any empirical study in which the goal is to make inferences about a population from a sample. In practice, the _________ used in a study is determined based on the expense of data collection, and the need to have sufficient statistical power.

   a. survey data
   b. Sample size
   c. The History and Present State of Electricity
   d. Divisia monetary aggregates index

2. _________ refers to an analytical process in which data, in both quantitative form (such as questionnaires results) or qualitative (such as interview transcripts) are categorised to facilitate analysis.

   _________ means the transformation of data into a form understandable by computer software. The classification of information is an important step in preparation of data for computer processing with statistical software.

   a. Social network change detection
   b. Probability sampling
   c. Coding
   d. Jantzen

3. . Analysis of data is a process of inspecting, cleaning, transforming, and modeling data with the goal of highlighting useful information, suggesting conclusions, and supporting decision making. _________ has multiple facets and approaches, encompassing diverse techniques under a variety of names, in different business, science, and social science domains.

   Data mining is a particular _________ technique that focuses on modeling and knowledge discovery for predictive rather than purely descriptive purposes.

   a. Data analysis

b. Scientific consensus
c. Selection bias
d. Probability sampling

4. In mathematics, a (real) _________ is a set of real numbers with the property that any number that lies between two numbers in the set is also included in the set. For example, the set of all numbers x satisfying $0 \le x \le 1$ is an _________ which contains 0 and 1, as well as all numbers between them. Other examples of _________s are the set of all real numbers $\mathbb{R}$, the set of all negative real numbers, and the empty set.

a. Open book decomposition
b. Interval
c. Dilution assay
d. Minimum viable population

5. In statistics, _________ refers to any statistical relationship between two random variables or two sets of data. Correlation refers to any of a broad class of statistical relationships involving _________.

Familiar examples of dependent phenomena include the correlation between the physical statures of parents and their offspring, and the correlation between the demand for a product and its price.

a. Correlational research
b. Dependence
c. Positive correlation
d. Probability sampling

ANSWER KEY
6. Presenting the Results of Quantitative Studies

---

1. b
2. c
3. a
4. b
5. b

---

7. Presenting the Results of Qualitative Research

CHAPTER OUTLINE: KEY TERMS, PEOPLE, PLACES, CONCEPTS

______ Coding

______ Data analysis

______ Phenomenology

______ Grounded theory

______ Axial coding

______ Constant

______ Hypothetico-deductive model

______ APA style

CHAPTER HIGHLIGHTS & NOTES: KEY TERMS, PEOPLE, PLACES, CONCEPTS

Coding

Coding refers to an analytical process in which data, in both quantitative form (such as questionnaires results) or qualitative (such as interview transcripts) are categorised to facilitate analysis.

Coding means the transformation of data into a form understandable by computer software. The classification of information is an important step in preparation of data for computer processing with statistical software.

Data analysis

Analysis of data is a process of inspecting, cleaning, transforming, and modeling data with the goal of highlighting useful information, suggesting conclusions, and supporting decision making. Data analysis has multiple facets and approaches, encompassing diverse techniques under a variety of names, in different business, science, and social science domains.

Data mining is a particular data analysis technique that focuses on modeling and knowledge discovery for predictive rather than purely descriptive purposes.

Phenomenology

The term phenomenology in science is used to describe a body of knowledge that relates empirical observations of phenomena to each other, in a way that is consistent with fundamental theory, but is not directly derived from theory.

For example, we find the following definition in the Concise Dictionary of Physics:'

Phenomenological Theory. A theory that expresses mathematically the results of observed phenomena without paying detailed attention to their fundamental significance.'

Grounded theory

Grounded theory method (GT) is a systematic methodology in the social sciences involving the discovery of theory through the analysis of data. It is mainly used in qualitative research, but is also applicable to quantitative data.

Grounded theory method is a research method, which operates almost in a reverse fashion from traditional research and at first sight may appear to be in contradiction to the scientific method.

Axial coding

Axial coding is the disaggregation of core themes during qualitative data analysis. Axial coding in Grounded Theory is the process of relating codes (categories and concepts) to each other, via a combination of inductive and deductive thinking. The basic framework of generic relationships is understood, according to Strauss and Corbin (1990, 1998) who propose the use of a 'coding paradigm', to include categories related to (1) the phenomenon under study, (2) the conditions related to that phenomenon (context conditions, intervening -structural- conditions or causal conditions), (3) the actions and interactional strategies directed at managing or handling the phenomenon and (4) the consequences of the actions/interactions related to the phenomenon.

Constant

In mathematics, a constant is a non-varying value, i.e. completely fixed or fixed in the context of use. The term usually occurs in opposition to variable (i.e. variable quantity), which is a symbol that stands for a value that may vary.

In polynomials, polynomial function of degree 2 is generally denoted as $ax^2 + bx + c,$

where a, b and c are constants , while x is the variable, a placeholder for the argument of the function being studied.

Hypothetico-deductive model

The hypothetico-deductive model, first so-named by William Whewell, is a proposed description of scientific method. According to it, scientific inquiry proceeds by formulating a hypothesis in a form that could conceivably be falsified by a test on observable data. A test that could and does run contrary to predictions of the hypothesis is taken as a falsification of the hypothesis.

APA style

American Psychological Association style is an academic format specified in The Publication Manual of the American Psychological Association, a style guide that offers academic authors guidance on various subjects for the submission of papers to the publications of APA. The APA states that the guidelines were developed to assist reading comprehension in the social and behavioral sciences, for clarity of communication, and for 'word choice that best reduces bias in language'. The Publication Manual of the American Psychological Association contains guidelines on many aspects of academic writing as it is seen appropriate by the APA.

7. Presenting the Results of Qualitative Research

CHAPTER HIGHLIGHTS & NOTES: KEY TERMS, PEOPLE, PLACES, CONCEPTS

Among the topics covered are information on the structure of research papers of various kinds, spelling rules, an author-date reference style, construction of tables and graphs, plagiarism, formatting of papers, and much more.

APA style is widely used, not only by APA publications but by various other scientific journals (including medical and public health journals), textbooks, and academia (for papers written in classes).

CHAPTER QUIZ: KEY TERMS, PEOPLE, PLACES, CONCEPTS

1. In mathematics, a _________ is a non-varying value, i.e. completely fixed or fixed in the context of use. The term usually occurs in opposition to variable (i.e. variable quantity), which is a symbol that stands for a value that may vary.

   In polynomials, polynomial function of degree 2 is generally denoted as $ax^2 + bx + c,$

   where a, b and c are _________s , while x is the variable, a placeholder for the argument of the function being studied.

   a. Direct relationship
   b. Function
   c. Magnitude
   d. Constant

2. The _________, first so-named by William Whewell, is a proposed description of scientific method. According to it, scientific inquiry proceeds by formulating a hypothesis in a form that could conceivably be falsified by a test on observable data. A test that could and does run contrary to predictions of the hypothesis is taken as a falsification of the hypothesis.

   a. Hypothetico-deductive model
   b. Law
   c. Medawar Lecture
   d. Mediocrity principle

3. . _________ is the disaggregation of core themes during qualitative data analysis. _________ in Grounded Theory is the process of relating codes (categories and concepts) to each other, via a combination of inductive and deductive thinking. The basic framework of generic relationships is understood, according to Strauss and Corbin (1990, 1998) who propose the use of a 'coding paradigm', to include categories related to (1) the phenomenon under study, (2) the conditions related to that phenomenon (context conditions, intervening -structural- conditions or causal conditions), (3) the actions and interactional strategies directed at managing or handling the phenomenon and (4) the consequences of the actions/interactions related to the phenomenon.

a. American Association for Public Opinion Research
b. Comparative historical research
c. Person-centered ethnography
d. Axial coding

4. Analysis of data is a process of inspecting, cleaning, transforming, and modeling data with the goal of highlighting useful information, suggesting conclusions, and supporting decision making. _________ has multiple facets and approaches, encompassing diverse techniques under a variety of names, in different business, science, and social science domains.

   Data mining is a particular _________ technique that focuses on modeling and knowledge discovery for predictive rather than purely descriptive purposes.

   a. Mertonian norms
   b. Data analysis
   c. Selection bias
   d. Probability sampling

5. _________ refers to an analytical process in which data, in both quantitative form (such as questionnaires results) or qualitative (such as interview transcripts) are categorised to facilitate analysis.

   _________ means the transformation of data into a form understandable by computer software. The classification of information is an important step in preparation of data for computer processing with statistical software.

   a. Social network change detection
   b. Probability sampling
   c. The History and Present State of Electricity
   d. Coding

ANSWER KEY
7. Presenting the Results of Qualitative Research

---

1. d
2. a
3. d
4. b
5. d

---

8. Discussion

CHAPTER OUTLINE: KEY TERMS, PEOPLE, PLACES, CONCEPTS

_______________ Element

_______________ Argument

_______________ Abstract

CHAPTER HIGHLIGHTS & NOTES: KEY TERMS, PEOPLE, PLACES, CONCEPTS

Element

In mathematics, an element or member of a set is any one of the distinct objects that make up that set.

Writing A = {1, 2, 3, 4 },means that the elements of the set A are the numbers 1, 2, 3 and 4. Sets of elements of A, for example {1, 2}, are subsets of A.

Sets can themselves be elements. For example consider the set B = {1, 2, {3, 4}}.

Argument

In logic and philosophy, an argument is an attempt to persuade someone of something, by giving reasons for accepting a particular conclusion as evident. The general structure of an argument in a natural language is that of premises (typically in the form of propositions, statements or sentences) in support of a claim: the conclusion. The structure of some arguments can also be set out in a formal language, and formally-defined 'arguments' can be made independently of natural language arguments, as in math, logic and computer science.

Abstract

An abstract is a brief summary of a research article, thesis, review, conference proceeding or any in-depth analysis of a particular subject or discipline, and is often used to help the reader quickly ascertain the paper's purpose. When used, an abstract always appears at the beginning of a manuscript or typescript, acting as the point-of-entry for any given academic paper or patent application. Abstracting and indexing services for various academic disciplines are aimed at compiling a body of literature for that particular subject.

1. In mathematics, an _________ or member of a set is any one of the distinct objects that make up that set.

   Writing A = {1, 2, 3, 4 },means that the _________s of the set A are the numbers 1, 2, 3 and 4. Sets of _________s of A, for example {1, 2}, are subsets of A.

   Sets can themselves be _________s. For example consider the set B = {1, 2, {3, 4}}.

   a. Empty function
   b. Element
   c. Identity function
   d. Image

2. In logic and philosophy, an _________ is an attempt to persuade someone of something, by giving reasons for accepting a particular conclusion as evident. The general structure of an _________ in a natural language is that of premises (typically in the form of propositions, statements or sentences) in support of a claim: the conclusion. The structure of some _________s can also be set out in a formal language, and formally-defined '_________s' can be made independently of natural language _________s, as in math, logic and computer science.

   a. Bounded function
   b. Argument
   c. Complex analytic geometry
   d. Conformal welding

3. An _________ is a brief summary of a research article, thesis, review, conference proceeding or any in-depth analysis of a particular subject or discipline, and is often used to help the reader quickly ascertain the paper's purpose. When used, an _________ always appears at the beginning of a manuscript or typescript, acting as the point-of-entry for any given academic paper or patent application. Abstracting and indexing services for various academic disciplines are aimed at compiling a body of literature for that particular subject.

   a. IMRAD
   b. American Association for Public Opinion Research
   c. Abstract
   d. Conformal welding

ANSWER KEY
8. Discussion

1. b
2. b
3. c

---

9. Overcoming Barriers: Becoming an Expert While Controlling Your Own D

CHAPTER OUTLINE: KEY TERMS, PEOPLE, PLACES, CONCEPTS

_______________	Axiology
_______________	Time management
_______________	Data analysis
_______________	Dependence
_______________	Coding
_______________	Reliability
_______________	Argument
_______________	Authorship
_______________	Case studies
_______________	Hypothetico-deductive model

CHAPTER HIGHLIGHTS & NOTES: KEY TERMS, PEOPLE, PLACES, CONCEPTS

Axiology	Axiology is the philosophical study of value. It is either the collective term for ethics and aesthetics--philosophical fields that depend crucially on notions of value--or the foundation for these fields, and thus similar to value theory and meta-ethics. The term was first used in the early 20th century by Paul Lapie, in 1902, and E. von Hartmann, in 1908.
Time management	Time management is the act or process of planning and exercising conscious control over the amount of time spent on specific activities, especially to increase effectiveness, efficiency or productivity. Time management may be aided by a range of skills, tools, and techniques used to manage time when accomplishing specific tasks, projects and goals complying with a due date. Initially, time management referred to just business or work activities, but eventually the term broadened to include personal activities as well.
Data analysis	Analysis of data is a process of inspecting, cleaning, transforming, and modeling data with the goal of highlighting useful information, suggesting conclusions, and supporting decision making.

Data analysis has multiple facets and approaches, encompassing diverse techniques under a variety of names, in different business, science, and social science domains.

Data mining is a particular data analysis technique that focuses on modeling and knowledge discovery for predictive rather than purely descriptive purposes.

Dependence

In statistics, dependence refers to any statistical relationship between two random variables or two sets of data. Correlation refers to any of a broad class of statistical relationships involving dependence.

Familiar examples of dependent phenomena include the correlation between the physical statures of parents and their offspring, and the correlation between the demand for a product and its price.

Coding

Coding refers to an analytical process in which data, in both quantitative form (such as questionnaires results) or qualitative (such as interview transcripts) are categorised to facilitate analysis.

Coding means the transformation of data into a form understandable by computer software. The classification of information is an important step in preparation of data for computer processing with statistical software.

Reliability

In statistics, reliability refers to the consistency of a measure. A measure is said to have a high reliability if it produces consistent results under consistent conditions. For example, measurements of people's height and weight are often extremely reliable.

Argument

In logic and philosophy, an argument is an attempt to persuade someone of something, by giving reasons for accepting a particular conclusion as evident. The general structure of an argument in a natural language is that of premises (typically in the form of propositions, statements or sentences) in support of a claim: the conclusion. The structure of some arguments can also be set out in a formal language, and formally-defined 'arguments' can be made independently of natural language arguments, as in math, logic and computer science.

Authorship

An author is broadly defined as 'the person who originated or gave existence to anything' and whose authorship determines responsibility for what was created. Narrowly defined, an author is the originator of any written work.

Case studies

In the social sciences and life sciences, a case study is a descriptive or explanatory analysis of a person, group or event. An explanatory case study is used to explore causation in order to find underlying principles. Case studies may be prospective (in which criteria are established and cases fitting the criteria are included as they become available) or retrospective (in which criteria are established for selecting cases from historical records for inclusion in the study).

9. Overcoming Barriers: Becoming an Expert While Controlling Your Own Des ...

CHAPTER HIGHLIGHTS & NOTES: KEY TERMS, PEOPLE, PLACES, CONCEPTS

Hypothetico-deductive model	The hypothetico-deductive model, first so-named by William Whewell, is a proposed description of scientific method. According to it, scientific inquiry proceeds by formulating a hypothesis in a form that could conceivably be falsified by a test on observable data. A test that could and does run contrary to predictions of the hypothesis is taken as a falsification of the hypothesis.

CHAPTER QUIZ: KEY TERMS, PEOPLE, PLACES, CONCEPTS

1. _________ is the philosophical study of value. It is either the collective term for ethics and aesthetics--philosophical fields that depend crucially on notions of value--or the foundation for these fields, and thus similar to value theory and meta-ethics. The term was first used in the early 20th century by Paul Lapie, in 1902, and E. von Hartmann, in 1908.

   a. Oblivion
   b. Axiology
   c. Extrinsic finality
   d. Animistic fallacy

2. The _________, first so-named by William Whewell, is a proposed description of scientific method. According to it, scientific inquiry proceeds by formulating a hypothesis in a form that could conceivably be falsified by a test on observable data. A test that could and does run contrary to predictions of the hypothesis is taken as a falsification of the hypothesis.

   a. Lakatos Award
   b. Law
   c. Medawar Lecture
   d. Hypothetico-deductive model

3. An author is broadly defined as 'the person who originated or gave existence to anything' and whose _________ determines responsibility for what was created. Narrowly defined, an author is the originator of any written work.

   a. American Association for Public Opinion Research
   b. Cauchy's integral theorem
   c. Authorship
   d. Conformal welding

4. . In the social sciences and life sciences, a _________(ies) is a descriptive or explanatory analysis of a person, group or event. An explanatory _________(ies) is used to explore causation in order to find underlying principles. _________ may be prospective (in which criteria are established and cases fitting the criteria are included as they become available) or retrospective (in which criteria are established for selecting cases from historical records for inclusion in the study).

   a. Probability sampling

b. Cauchy's integral theorem
c. Complex analytic geometry
d. Case studies

5. _________ refers to an analytical process in which data, in both quantitative form (such as questionnaires results) or qualitative (such as interview transcripts) are categorised to facilitate analysis.

   _________ means the transformation of data into a form understandable by computer software. The classification of information is an important step in preparation of data for computer processing with statistical software.

   a. Coding
   b. Linear relationship
   c. Positive correlation
   d. Probability sampling

ANSWER KEY

9. Overcoming Barriers: Becoming an Expert While Controlling Your Own Des ...

1. b
2. d
3. c
4. d
5. a

---

10. Writing

CHAPTER OUTLINE: KEY TERMS, PEOPLE, PLACES, CONCEPTS

____________	Authorship
____________	Frequency
____________	Frequency distribution
____________	Mode
____________	Publication Manual of the American Psychological Association
____________	External validity
____________	Validity

CHAPTER HIGHLIGHTS & NOTES: KEY TERMS, PEOPLE, PLACES, CONCEPTS

Authorship

An author is broadly defined as 'the person who originated or gave existence to anything' and whose authorship determines responsibility for what was created. Narrowly defined, an author is the originator of any written work.

Frequency

In statistics the frequency of an event i is the number n_i of times the event occurred in the experiment or the study. These frequencies are often graphically represented in histograms.

We speak of absolute frequencies, when the counts n_i themselves are given and of (relative) frequencies, when those are normalized by the total number of events: $f_i = \frac{n_i}{N} = \frac{n_i}{\sum_i n_i}.$

Taking the f_i for all i and tabulating or plotting them leads to a frequency distribution.

Frequency distribution

In statistics, a frequency distribution is an arrangement of the values that one or more variables take in a sample. Each entry in the table contains the frequency or count of the occurrences of values within a particular group or interval, and in this way, the table summarizes the distribution of values in the sample.

Mode

In statistics, the mode is the value that occurs most frequently in a data set or a probability distribution.

In some fields, notably education, sample data are often called scores, and the sample mode is known as the modal score.

Like the statistical mean and median, the mode is a way of capturing important information about a random variable or a population in a single quantity.

Publication Manual of the American Psychological Association	American Psychological Association style is an academic format specified in The Publication Manual of the American Psychological Association, a style guide that offers academic authors guidance on various subjects for the submission of papers to the publications of APA. The APA states that the guidelines were developed to assist reading comprehension in the social and behavioral sciences, for clarity of communication, and for 'word choice that best reduces bias in language'. The Publication Manual of the American Psychological Association contains guidelines on many aspects of academic writing as it is seen appropriate by the APA. Among the topics covered are information on the structure of research papers of various kinds, spelling rules, an author-date reference style, construction of tables and graphs, plagiarism, formatting of papers, and much more.
External validity	External validity is the validity of generalized (causal) inferences in scientific studies, usually based on experiments as experimental validity. Inferences about cause-effect relationships based on a specific scientific study are said to possess external validity if they may be generalized from the unique and idiosyncratic settings, procedures and participants to other populations and conditions. Causal inferences said to possess high degrees of external validity can reasonably be expected to apply (a) to the target population of the study (i.e. from which the sample was drawn) (also referred to as population validity), and (b) to the universe of other populations (e.g. across time and space).
Validity	In science and statistics, validity has no single agreed definition but generally refers to the extent to which a concept, conclusion or measurement is well-founded and corresponds accurately to the real world. The word 'valid' is derived from the Latin validus, meaning strong. The validity of a measurement tool (for example, a test in education) is considered to be the degree to which the tool measures what it claims to measure.

10. Writing

CHAPTER QUIZ: KEY TERMS, PEOPLE, PLACES, CONCEPTS

1. In statistics, a _________ is an arrangement of the values that one or more variables take in a sample. Each entry in the table contains the frequency or count of the occurrences of values within a particular group or interval, and in this way, the table summarizes the distribution of values in the sample.

   a. Generalized entropy index
   b. Gini coefficient
   c. Hoover index
   d. Frequency distribution

2. In statistics the _________ of an event i is the number n_i of times the event occurred in the experiment or the study. These _________(ies) are often graphically represented in histograms.

   We speak of absolute _________(ies), when the counts n_i themselves are given and of (relative) _________(ies), when those are normalized by the total number of events: $f_i = \frac{n_i}{N} = \frac{n_i}{\sum_i n_i}.$

   Taking the f_i for all i and tabulating or plotting them leads to a _________ distribution.

   a. Frequency
   b. Generalized entropy index
   c. Gini coefficient
   d. Hoover index

3. In statistics, the _________ is the value that occurs most frequently in a data set or a probability distribution. In some fields, notably education, sample data are often called scores, and the sample _________ is known as the modal score.

   Like the statistical mean and median, the _________ is a way of capturing important information about a random variable or a population in a single quantity.

   a. Nonparametric skew
   b. Mode
   c. Polychoric correlation
   d. Range

4. . American Psychological Association style is an academic format specified in The _________, a style guide that offers academic authors guidance on various subjects for the submission of papers to the publications of APA. The APA states that the guidelines were developed to assist reading comprehension in the social and behavioral sciences, for clarity of communication, and for 'word choice that best reduces bias in language'. The _________ contains guidelines on many aspects of academic writing as it is seen appropriate by the APA. Among the topics covered are information on the structure of research papers of various kinds, spelling rules, an author-date reference style, construction of tables and graphs, plagiarism, formatting of papers, and much more.

a. PsycINFO
b. Publication Manual of the American Psychological Association
c. Probability sampling
d. The History and Present State of Electricity

5. An author is broadly defined as 'the person who originated or gave existence to anything' and whose _________ determines responsibility for what was created. Narrowly defined, an author is the originator of any written work.

a. American Association for Public Opinion Research
b. Authorship
c. A. Edward Nussbaum
d. I-bundle

ANSWER KEY
10. Writing

1. d
2. a
3. b
4. b
5. b

CHAPTER OUTLINE: KEY TERMS, PEOPLE, PLACES, CONCEPTS

Census

Data collection

Institute for Social Research

Inter-university Consortium for Political and Social Research

Secondary data

Collection

Data analysis

Justice

National Longitudinal Surveys

Proquest

Hypothetico-deductive model

Survey research

Dependence

CHAPTER HIGHLIGHTS & NOTES: KEY TERMS, PEOPLE, PLACES, CONCEPTS

Census	A census is the procedure of systematically acquiring and recording information about the members of a given population. It is a regularly occurring and official count of a particular population. The term is used mostly in connection with national population and housing censuses; other common censuses include agriculture, business, and traffic censuses.
Data collection	Data collection is any process of preparing and collecting data, for example, as part of a process improvement or similar project. The purpose of data collection is to obtain information to keep on record, to make decisions about important issues, or to pass information on to others. Data are primarily collected to provide information regarding a specific topic.
Institute for Social Research	The Institute for Social Research is a research organization for sociology and continental philosophy, best known as the institutional home of the Frankfurt School and critical theory. The Institute was founded in Frankfurt am Main in 1923, where it was (and as of 2005 once again is) affiliated with the University of Frankfurt am Main. It was founded by Felix Weil, a student of the Marxian philosopher Karl Korsch, with an endowment provided by Weil's wealthy father Hermann Weil.
Inter-university Consortium for Political and Social Research	ICPSR, the Inter-university Consortium for Political and Social Research, was established in 1962. An integral part of the infrastructure of social science research, ICPSR maintains and provides access to a vast archive of social science data for research and instruction (over 8,000 discrete studies/surveys with more than 60,000 datasets), and offers training in quantitative methods to facilitate effective data use. To ensure that data resources are available to future generations of scholars, ICPSR preserves data, migrating them to new storage media as changes in technology warrant. In addition, ICPSR provides user support to assist researchers in identifying relevant data for analysis and in conducting their research projects.
Secondary data	Secondary data, is data collected by someone other than the user. Common sources of secondary data for social science include censuses, organizational records and data collected through qualitative methodologies or qualitative research. Primary data, by contrast, are collected by the investigator conducting the research.
Collection	In computer science, a collection is a grouping of some variable number of data items (possibly zero) that have some shared significance to the problem being solved and need to be operated upon together in some controlled fashion. Generally, the data items will be of the same type or, in languages supporting inheritance, derived from some common ancestor type. A table is usually not considered a collection because it holds a fixed number of items, although tables/arrays commonly play a role in the implementation of collections.
Data analysis	Analysis of data is a process of inspecting, cleaning, transforming, and modeling data with the goal of highlighting useful information, suggesting conclusions, and supporting decision making.

Data analysis has multiple facets and approaches, encompassing diverse techniques under a variety of names, in different business, science, and social science domains.

Data mining is a particular data analysis technique that focuses on modeling and knowledge discovery for predictive rather than purely descriptive purposes.

Justice	Justice in economics is a subcategory of welfare economics with models frequently representing the ethical-social requirements of a given theory, whether 'in the large,' as of a just social order, or 'in the small,' as in the equity of 'how institutions distribute specific benefits and burdens.' That theory may or may not elicit acceptance. In the Journal of Economic Literature classification codes 'justice' is scrolled to at JEL: D63, wedged on the same line between 'Equity' and 'Inequality' along with 'Other Normative Criteria and Measurement'. Categories above and below the line are Externalities and Altruism.
National Longitudinal Surveys	The National Longitudinal Surveys are a set of surveys conducted by the US Department of Labor's Bureau of Labor Statistics, designed to gather information at multiple points in time on significant life events of several population samples of US citizens, especially their labor market activities.
Proquest	ProQuest LLC is an Ann Arbor, Michigan-based electronic publisher and microfilm publisher. It provides archives of sources such as newspapers, periodicals, dissertations, and aggregated databases of many types. Its content is estimated at 125 billion digital pages.
Hypothetico-deductive model	The hypothetico-deductive model, first so-named by William Whewell, is a proposed description of scientific method. According to it, scientific inquiry proceeds by formulating a hypothesis in a form that could conceivably be falsified by a test on observable data. A test that could and does run contrary to predictions of the hypothesis is taken as a falsification of the hypothesis.
Survey research	Survey research This method was pioneered in the 1930s and 1940s by sociologist Paul Lazarsfeld. The initial use of the method was to examine the effects of the radio on political opinion formation of the United States. One of its early successes was the development of the theory of two-step flow of communication.
Dependence	In statistics, dependence refers to any statistical relationship between two random variables or two sets of data. Correlation refers to any of a broad class of statistical relationships involving dependence. Familiar examples of dependent phenomena include the correlation between the physical statures of parents and their offspring, and the correlation between the demand for a product and its price.

CHAPTER QUIZ: KEY TERMS, PEOPLE, PLACES, CONCEPTS

1. In computer science, a _________ is a grouping of some variable number of data items (possibly zero) that have some shared significance to the problem being solved and need to be operated upon together in some controlled fashion. Generally, the data items will be of the same type or, in languages supporting inheritance, derived from some common ancestor type. A table is usually not considered a _________ because it holds a fixed number of items, although tables/arrays commonly play a role in the implementation of _________s.

   a. Container
   b. Piece table
   c. Collection
   d. Zipper

2. The _________ is a research organization for sociology and continental philosophy, best known as the institutional home of the Frankfurt School and critical theory.

   The Institute was founded in Frankfurt am Main in 1923, where it was (and as of 2005 once again is) affiliated with the University of Frankfurt am Main. It was founded by Felix Weil, a student of the Marxian philosopher Karl Korsch, with an endowment provided by Weil's wealthy father Hermann Weil.

   a. Institute for Social Research
   b. multivariate analysis of variance
   c. International Geosphere-Biosphere Programme
   d. A. Edward Nussbaum

3. A _________ is the procedure of systematically acquiring and recording information about the members of a given population. It is a regularly occurring and official count of a particular population. The term is used mostly in connection with national population and housing _________es; other common _________es include agriculture, business, and traffic _________es.

   a. Census
   b. The History and Present State of Electricity
   c. Essay on the Inequality of the Human Races
   d. Jantzen

4. . ICPSR, the _________, was established in 1962. An integral part of the infrastructure of social science research, ICPSR maintains and provides access to a vast archive of social science data for research and instruction (over 8,000 discrete studies/surveys with more than 60,000 datasets), and offers training in quantitative methods to facilitate effective data use. To ensure that data resources are available to future generations of scholars, ICPSR preserves data, migrating them to new storage media as changes in technology warrant. In addition, ICPSR provides user support to assist researchers in identifying relevant data for analysis and in conducting their research projects.

   a. Inter-university Consortium for Political and Social Research
   b. multivariate analysis of variance
   c. International Geosphere-Biosphere Programme

5. _________ is any process of preparing and collecting data, for example, as part of a process improvement or similar project. The purpose of _________ is to obtain information to keep on record, to make decisions about important issues, or to pass information on to others. Data are primarily collected to provide information regarding a specific topic.

   a. MANOVA
   b. multivariate analysis of variance
   c. Probability sampling
   d. Data collection

ANSWER KEY

11. How to Complete Your Dissertation Using Online Data Access and Collect ...

---

1. c

2. a

3. a

4. a

5. d

---

12. Guidelines for the Presentation of Numbers in the Dissertation

CHAPTER OUTLINE: KEY TERMS, PEOPLE, PLACES, CONCEPTS

______ APA style

______ Publication Manual of the American Psychological Association

______ Authorship

CHAPTER HIGHLIGHTS & NOTES: KEY TERMS, PEOPLE, PLACES, CONCEPTS

APA style

American Psychological Association style is an academic format specified in The Publication Manual of the American Psychological Association, a style guide that offers academic authors guidance on various subjects for the submission of papers to the publications of APA. The APA states that the guidelines were developed to assist reading comprehension in the social and behavioral sciences, for clarity of communication, and for 'word choice that best reduces bias in language'. The Publication Manual of the American Psychological Association contains guidelines on many aspects of academic writing as it is seen appropriate by the APA. Among the topics covered are information on the structure of research papers of various kinds, spelling rules, an author-date reference style, construction of tables and graphs, plagiarism, formatting of papers, and much more.

APA style is widely used, not only by APA publications but by various other scientific journals (including medical and public health journals), textbooks, and academia (for papers written in classes).

Publication Manual of the American Psychological Association

American Psychological Association style is an academic format specified in The Publication Manual of the American Psychological Association, a style guide that offers academic authors guidance on various subjects for the submission of papers to the publications of APA. The APA states that the guidelines were developed to assist reading comprehension in the social and behavioral sciences, for clarity of communication, and for 'word choice that best reduces bias in language'. The Publication Manual of the American Psychological Association contains guidelines on many aspects of academic writing as it is seen appropriate by the APA. Among the topics covered are information on the structure of research papers of various kinds, spelling rules, an author-date reference style, construction of tables and graphs, plagiarism, formatting of papers, and much more.

Authorship

An author is broadly defined as 'the person who originated or gave existence to anything' and whose authorship determines responsibility for what was created.

12. Guidelines for the Presentation of Numbers in the Dissertation

CHAPTER QUIZ: KEY TERMS, PEOPLE, PLACES, CONCEPTS

1. American Psychological Association style is an academic format specified in The Publication Manual of the American Psychological Association, a style guide that offers academic authors guidance on various subjects for the submission of papers to the publications of APA. The APA states that the guidelines were developed to assist reading comprehension in the social and behavioral sciences, for clarity of communication, and for 'word choice that best reduces bias in language'. The Publication Manual of the American Psychological Association contains guidelines on many aspects of academic writing as it is seen appropriate by the APA. Among the topics covered are information on the structure of research papers of various kinds, spelling rules, an author-date reference style, construction of tables and graphs, plagiarism, formatting of papers, and much more.

   _________ is widely used, not only by APA publications but by various other scientific journals (including medical and public health journals), textbooks, and academia (for papers written in classes).

   a. American Association for Public Opinion Research
   b. APA style
   c. A. Edward Nussbaum
   d. I-bundle

2. American Psychological Association style is an academic format specified in The _________, a style guide that offers academic authors guidance on various subjects for the submission of papers to the publications of APA. The APA states that the guidelines were developed to assist reading comprehension in the social and behavioral sciences, for clarity of communication, and for 'word choice that best reduces bias in language'. The _________ contains guidelines on many aspects of academic writing as it is seen appropriate by the APA. Among the topics covered are information on the structure of research papers of various kinds, spelling rules, an author-date reference style, construction of tables and graphs, plagiarism, formatting of papers, and much more.

   a. PsycINFO
   b. Publication Manual of the American Psychological Association
   c. Probability sampling
   d. The History and Present State of Electricity

3. An author is broadly defined as 'the person who originated or gave existence to anything' and whose _________ determines responsibility for what was created. Narrowly defined, an author is the originator of any written work.

   a. American Association for Public Opinion Research
   b. Publication Manual of the American Psychological Association
   c. Authorship
   d. The History and Present State of Electricity

ANSWER KEY
12. Guidelines for the Presentation of Numbers in the Dissertation

1. b
2. b
3. c

---

13. Informed Consent and Other Ethical Concerns

CHAPTER OUTLINE: KEY TERMS, PEOPLE, PLACES, CONCEPTS

- Census
- Institutional review boards
- Validity
- Inferential statistics
- Research design
- Case studies
- Element
- Informed consent
- Accountability
- Bias
- Authorship
- Free writing
- Research ethics

13. Informed Consent and Other Ethical Concerns

CHAPTER HIGHLIGHTS & NOTES: KEY TERMS, PEOPLE, PLACES, CONCEPTS

Census

A census is the procedure of systematically acquiring and recording information about the members of a given population. It is a regularly occurring and official count of a particular population. The term is used mostly in connection with national population and housing censuses; other common censuses include agriculture, business, and traffic censuses.

Institutional review boards

An institutional review board, also known as an independent ethics committee or ethical review board, is a committee that has been formally designated to approve, monitor, and review biomedical and behavioral research involving humans. They often conduct some form of risk-benefit analysis in an attempt to determine whether or not research should be done. The number one priority of Institutional review boardss is to protect human subjects from physical or psychological harm.

Validity

In science and statistics, validity has no single agreed definition but generally refers to the extent to which a concept, conclusion or measurement is well-founded and corresponds accurately to the real world. The word 'valid' is derived from the Latin validus, meaning strong. The validity of a measurement tool (for example, a test in education) is considered to be the degree to which the tool measures what it claims to measure.

Inferential statistics

In statistics, statistical inference is the process of drawing conclusions from data that is subject to random variation, for example, observational errors or sampling variation. More substantially, the terms statistical inference, statistical induction and inferential statistics are used to describe systems of procedures that can be used to draw conclusions from datasets arising from systems affected by random variation, such as observational errors, random sampling, or random experimentation. Initial requirements of such a system of procedures for inference and induction are that the system should produce reasonable answers when applied to well-defined situations and that it should be general enough to be applied across a range of situations.

Research design

Research design is considered as a 'blueprint' for research, dealing with at least four problems: which questions to study, which data are relevant, what data to collect, and how to analyze the results.. The best design depends on the research question as well as the orientation of the researcher. Every design has its positive and negative sides.

Case studies

In the social sciences and life sciences, a case study is a descriptive or explanatory analysis of a person, group or event. An explanatory case study is used to explore causation in order to find underlying principles. Case studies may be prospective (in which criteria are established and cases fitting the criteria are included as they become available) or retrospective (in which criteria are established for selecting cases from historical records for inclusion in the study).

Element

In mathematics, an element or member of a set is any one of the distinct objects that make up that set.

Writing $A = \{1, 2, 3, 4\}$,means that the elements of the set A are the numbers 1, 2, 3 and 4.

Sets of elements of A, for example {1, 2}, are subsets of A.

Sets can themselves be elements. For example consider the set B = {1, 2, {3, 4}}.

Informed consent

Informed consent is a process for getting permission before conducting a healthcare intervention on a person. A health care provider may ask a patient to consent to receive therapy before providing it, or a clinical researcher may ask a research participant before enrolling that person into a clinical trial. Informed consent is collected according to guidelines from the fields of medical ethics and research ethics.

Accountability

In ethics and governance, accountability is answerability, blameworthiness, liability, and the expectation of account-giving. As an aspect of governance, it has been central to discussions related to problems in the public sector, nonprofit and private (corporate) worlds. In leadership roles, accountability is the acknowledgment and assumption of responsibility for actions, products, decisions, and policies including the administration, governance, and implementation within the scope of the role or employment position and encompassing the obligation to report, explain and be answerable for resulting consequences.

Bias

A statistic is biased if it is calculated in such a way that is systematically different from the population parameter of interest. The following lists some types of, or aspects of, bias which should not be considered mutually exclusive:•Selection bias, where individuals or groups are more likely to take part in a research project than others, resulting in biased samples. This can also be termed Berksonian bias.

Authorship

An author is broadly defined as 'the person who originated or gave existence to anything' and whose authorship determines responsibility for what was created. Narrowly defined, an author is the originator of any written work.

Free writing

Free writing is a prewriting technique in which a person writes continuously for a set period of time without regard to spelling, grammar, or topic. It produces raw, often unusable material, but helps writers overcome blocks of apathy and self-criticism. It is used mainly by prose writers and writing teachers.

Research ethics

Research ethics involves the application of fundamental ethical principles to a variety of topics involving scientific research. These include the design and implementation of research involving human experimentation, animal experimentation, various aspects of academic scandal, including scientific misconduct (such as fraud, fabrication of data and plagiarism), whistleblowing; regulation of research, etc. Research ethics is most developed as a concept in medical research.

13. Informed Consent and Other Ethical Concerns

CHAPTER QUIZ: KEY TERMS, PEOPLE, PLACES, CONCEPTS

1. _________ is a prewriting technique in which a person writes continuously for a set period of time without regard to spelling, grammar, or topic. It produces raw, often unusable material, but helps writers overcome blocks of apathy and self-criticism. It is used mainly by prose writers and writing teachers.

   a. Probability sampling
   b. Coherence
   c. Completeness
   d. Free writing

2. An _________(s), also known as an independent ethics committee or ethical review board, is a committee that has been formally designated to approve, monitor, and review biomedical and behavioral research involving humans. They often conduct some form of risk-benefit analysis in an attempt to determine whether or not research should be done. The number one priority of Institutional review boardss is to protect human subjects from physical or psychological harm.

   a. Institutional review boards
   b. The History and Present State of Electricity
   c. Essay on the Inequality of the Human Races
   d. Jantzen

3. A _________ is the procedure of systematically acquiring and recording information about the members of a given population. It is a regularly occurring and official count of a particular population. The term is used mostly in connection with national population and housing _________es; other common _________es include agriculture, business, and traffic _________es.

   a. Probability sampling
   b. The History and Present State of Electricity
   c. Essay on the Inequality of the Human Races
   d. Census

4. In ethics and governance, _________ is answerability, blameworthiness, liability, and the expectation of account-giving. As an aspect of governance, it has been central to discussions related to problems in the public sector, nonprofit and private (corporate) worlds. In leadership roles, _________ is the acknowledgment and assumption of responsibility for actions, products, decisions, and policies including the administration, governance, and implementation within the scope of the role or employment position and encompassing the obligation to report, explain and be answerable for resulting consequences.

   a. American Association for Public Opinion Research
   b. Empty set
   c. Accountability
   d. Image

5. . In science and statistics, _________ has no single agreed definition but generally refers to the extent to which a concept, conclusion or measurement is well-founded and corresponds accurately to the real world. The word 'valid' is derived from the Latin validus, meaning strong. The _________ of a measurement tool (for example, a test in education) is considered to be the degree to which the tool measures what it claims to measure.

a. Vitalism
b. Validity
c. The History and Present State of Electricity
d. Jantzen

ANSWER KEY
13. Informed Consent and Other Ethical Concerns

1. d
2. a
3. d
4. c
5. b

Other Facts101 e-Books and Tests

CPSIA information can be obtained at www.ICGtesting.com
Printed in the USA
LVOW01s1620270114

371156LV00006B/482/P